Fly-Fishing
the North Country

Shawn Perich
Illustrated by David Minix

Pfeifer-Hamilton
Duluth, Minnesota

Pfeifer-Hamilton Publishers
210 West Michigan
Duluth MN 55802-1908 218-727-0500

Fly-Fishing the North Country

Printed in the United States of America by Versa Press.
10 9 8 7 6 5 4 3 2

Editorial Director: Susan Gustafson
Graphic Design: Jeff Brownell

Library of Congress Cataloging in Publication Data
94-74626

ISBN 1-57025-063-4

To my Mom, Terese Perich,
who once paid one of my hand-tied flies
the supreme compliment:
she swatted it.

Acknowledgments

The following persons generously provided their expertise to this book: Dave Asproth, Ed Atcas, Keith G. Baribeau, Keith Behn, Dick Berge, Carl Bradley, Greg Breining, Bob Cary, Larry Dahlberg, Eric DiCarlo, Walter Fowlie, Mike Furtman, Chuck Gritzner, Henry Haugley, Karl Kaufman, Ken Kettunen, Roger LaPenter, Al Larson, Richard W. Lenski, Fran Lisignoli, Alan Lutkevich, Ron Manz, Larry Meicher, Paul Morgan, Bob Nasby, Bruce Pomeroy, Perry Rowlison, Ron Shoberg, Erik Swenson, Reuben Swenson, Chris Timmerman, and Damian Wilmot.

Contents

Introduction

In this busy, noisy, impatient world, faster often seems better. Many of us wear stress like a badge of honor and take pride in exhaustion. Rising for work before dawn and returning home after dark—rarely taking time to enjoy the world around us—we easily lose touch with nature and with ourselves.

Perhaps we won't solve these problems by going fly-fishing. But I like to think it can't hurt. When we fly-fish, nature sets the pace. We can't program mayfly hatches nor can we force a fish to bite. Stream levels and weather conditions are out of our control. To fool fish with an artificial fly, we must become participants in the natural world. As we settle into the rhythm of the cast, our body relaxes and our mind clears.

Fly-fishing is the most artful expression of angling, a celebration of fishing. You don't have to catch fish to enjoy wading in a stream and casting a fly. Just being there is enough.

But lack of knowledge prevents many potential fly-fishers from getting started. They don't know where to go or what fish species they might catch. They aren't sure what equipment is essential for novices. This book will help you begin. It will show you how to select tackle, where to find fish, and how to catch them.

You don't have to travel to Montana for fly-fishing. Sure, the mountains are nice, but the north woods has plenty of fresh air and fine scenery plus some of the best fly-fishing you'll find anywhere. Don't believe it? Then try fishing for brown trout in the Bois Brule, smallmouth bass in the Boundary Waters or northern pike in the Ontario bush. Keep an open mind and you'll always find fresh fly-fishing challenges in north-country waters. Every northern game fish can be caught with a fly.

I hope you have as much fun reading this book as I had researching and writing it. The north woods may seem remote to editors of national fly-fishing magazines, yet I quickly discovered that the north country is populated with knowledgeable and innovative fly-fishers. I've never met kinder, more generous people than those who agreed to share their expertise with the readers of this book. They welcomed me into their homes, took me to their favorite fishing places, and shared with me their best fly patterns. Some are trout purists. Others like bass. A few pursue pike and muskies. Regardless of their tastes in fishing, they hold in common a respect for their sport and the beautiful places where they fish.

In the following chapters, you'll meet these fly-fishers and learn how they fish. Because this book is likely to be read by fly-fishers of varying skill levels, I've provided some basic how-to information to ensure we're all speaking the same language, and I've tried to keep the jargon and unnecessary technical talk to a minimum.

The flies mentioned in the book were recommended to me as ones that catch fish. The "north-country fly box" at the back of the book tells how to tie them. Some of these fly patterns have never before been featured in print.

The north country is a special place. Where else can you find fresh timber wolf tracks on a muddy portage or share a lake with a loon? Don't come to this country merely to catch fish. Take some time to get reaquainted with the world around you. Slow down, look and listen. Even if you don't catch anything, the change will do you good.

The First Cast

Fly-fishing made easy

Want to bring a north-country fishing conversation to an abrupt end? Start talking about fly-fishing. It's a subject sure to silence even the most rabid leech wrangler. Why? First, most north-woods anglers know little about fly-fishing. But perhaps more important, this wonderful sport has long been stereotyped as only for highbrows. Too often anglers stay away from fly-fishing because they assume you need a six-figure income and a master's degree to enjoy it. Nothing could be further from the truth. Fly-fishers come from all walks of life. About the only trait they share is an intense love of fishing. Fortunately, more folks are stepping past the stereotype and discovering fly-fishing. Anyone can do it. If you can walk and chew gum, you can fly-fish.

You don't need to learn the Latin names of bugs or read hundred-year-old fishing books to become a fly-fisher, but you must understand the basics of tackle and technique. In fact, you have to "speak the language" in order to read this book. Consider this chapter a crash course in fly-fishing basics. More detailed information is available in dozens of books and videos. You can also attend

Fly-fishers come from all walks of life. The trait they share is an intense love of fishing.

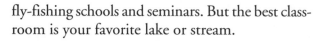

fly-fishing schools and seminars. But the best class-room is your favorite lake or stream.

Fly rods

Fighting butts

A fly reel attaches to the base of the fly rod. Some fly rods, particularly medium- and heavy-weight models, have a short, usually detachable extension called a fighting butt. The fighting butt gives you extra leverage for fighting big fish. It's also handy for keeping your fly reel out of the mud and sand if you must set down your fly rod.

Let's start our crash course with fly rods. Most modern fly rods are made of graphite or a similar high-tech material. You can find actions ranging from feather-light to super-heavy. Actions carry numbers to match the correct fly line, with low numbers for light rods and high numbers for heavy ones. A 4-weight rod is suited to casting tiny dry flies for small trout or bluegills, while a 12-weight will handle a strong saltwater fish. Most fly rods are seven to nine feet in length. Longer rods are easier to cast.

A beginner looking for an all-purpose north-woods rod will be well served by a 6-weight or 7-weight rod nine feet in length. Catching stream trout with such a rod is sporty, but the rod also has the backbone to cast larger flies necessary for fish such as smallmouth bass. However, medium- and heavy-weight rods do a better job of casting bass bugs, streamers, and other bulky flies that are used to entice big fish.

A fly rod will be the most expensive purchase you'll make as a beginner, but it needn't break the bank. Most rod manufacturers offer excellent in-expensive models. Shop around. Not only will you find the best buy, but you may learn something about fly rods as well. If you decide you enjoy fly-fishing, you can always purchase a more expensive rod later. Store your fly rod in a case whenever it's not in use, to prevent breakage.

Fly lines

Next, you should select a line. Fly lines are num-bered to match fly rods, with low numbers signifying light weights and high numbers heavy ones. You would match a #7 fly line to a 7-weight fly rod. That's easy enough, but understanding fly line tapers is a little more tricky. Fly lines taper from thin ends to a thick midsection so they lay out gently on the water. Some lines, called double-tapers, taper on both ends, so you can reverse the line when the first end wears out. Others, called weight-forwards, have more weight in the first thirty feet or so to make casting easier.

What line should you buy? Well, you get more bang for your buck with a double-taper. If you plan to spend most of your time fishing with smaller flies for species such as trout or bluegills, a double-taper will serve you well. If you're after bass and pike, then go with a weight-forward which is best suited to casting big flies. Many trout anglers prefer weight-forward lines for long casts and fishing on breezy days. Weight-forward lines are available in a variety of tapers, so make sure you understand the manufacturer's nomenclature before you purchase one. Fly lines are encoded in the following manner: line type, weight, floating or sinking. For example, a package coded WF5F means that the line is a weight-forward, 5-weight that floats. A line marked DT7S is a double taper, 7-weight that sinks.

Fly lines come in both floating and sinking models, but most beginners choose floating lines because they are more versatile. A floating fly line suffices for most situations part-time fly-fishers encounter. You can use a floating line to fish flies on the surface and below. Floating lines are easy to control in stream currents. If you were to purchase just one fly line, a weight-forward floater would be a good choice.

Manufacturers offer a sophisticated array of sinking fly lines designed to perform specific tasks. You can get lines that sink just beneath the surface

Fly line recommendations

- Use a floating double-taper or a sink-tip line for trout in streams.

- Carry floating, intermediate, and full-sinking weight-forward lines for fishing in lakes.

- A floating weight-forward line works well for bass and pike.

Shooting head

To make a shooting head, tie a loop in the end of the running line and in the end of the sinking line. Then interlace the two loops.

Form a loop in the end of each line.

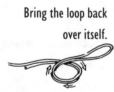

Bring the loop back over itself.

Wrap the loop around twice.

Pull tight.

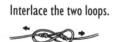

Interlace the two loops.

Pull tight.

or ones that drop to depths of twenty-five feet or more. Serious north-woods anglers are discovering that sinking fly lines add another dimension to fishing because you can use them to probe far beneath the surface of lakes.

The slowest sinking lines, called intermediates, are popular with lake anglers because they stay close to the surface, yet are unaffected by wave action. Most manufacturers offer several graduations of full-sinking lines, so you can fish a wide range of depths. If you know the line's sink rate, you can cast and then count down to reach a specific depth.

Sink-tip lines are a compromise between floating and sinking lines. The forward portion of the line sinks, but the rest of the length floats. Stream anglers prefer sink tips, because they are easier to control in currents. Sink-tips also come in graduations ranging from slow sinking to fast sinking. You can trim the length of the sinking portion to modify the line's performance.

Some anglers use a shooting head system to inexpensively develop a range of sinking fly lines. A shooting head is a section of fly line about thirty feet long, followed by a thin running line. Shooting heads were first developed for long-distance casting. Casting the shooting head like a projectile, the angler "shoots" the running line. You can buy shooting heads or make two of your own by cutting a double-taper fly line in half. All you need is one reel spool loaded with running line, because you can attach various shooting heads using a loop-to-loop system.

Fly reels

The fly reel is the least important part of your outfit, because all it does is store the line. Most fly reels are single action, which means the spool makes one revolution for each turn of the handle. Occasionally you'll see spring-operated automatic reels, which retrieve line when you press a lever.

What are qualities to look for in a good reel? Choose one that has a sensitive drag setting for fishing with light leaders. Many anglers prefer single-action reels with an exposed spool rim so they can apply drag with their palm. If you plan to use more than one fly line, look for a reel that has affordable spare spools. Many excellent, moderately priced fly reels are on the market. Pick one you can afford that looks durable enough to last a lifetime.

Fly reel

Leader logic

Are you now ready to start fishing? Not quite. Buy a couple of tapered monofilament leaders. The leader connects the fly line to the fly. It is heavier on the butt end, where it attaches to the line, and lighter on the tippet, where you tie on the fly. Leaders come in lengths varying from 7 1/2 feet to 12 feet or more. Dry fly anglers use long leaders so that wary trout don't see the heavy fly line. A beginner can get by with the 7 1/2- or 9-footers typically sold in fishing shops. Experienced anglers make their own leaders to meet their needs in various fishing situations.

How strong should your leader be? Well, you have to learn a little more jargon. Leaders are measured by the diameter and pound-test of the tippet. However, the packaging is coded with a number followed by an X. What does that mean? Simply put, the lower the number, the heavier the leader. Use a 2X leader for bass and a 6X leader for wary stream trout. A 4X leader makes a good choice for a beginner who's planning an excursion to the nearest bluegill pond. If you are lucky enough to be at a fly shop, ask the clerk to show you how to tie the leader to the fly line. Otherwise, use the knot recommended on the leader package.

Fishing on the lawn

OK, you've got the gear. Now let's put it to use. Unless you have easy access to a pond or lake, make the first casts with your new outfit on the lawn. Don't worry if the neighbors stare; the ease of practicing in an open area is worth a few snickers. Fly-casting is simply a matter of timing. Remember, you are casting the weight of the line, not the lure. Most beginners mess up because they cast too fast. Slow down and concentrate on fluid

You're among friends

The best way to learn about fly-fishing is to spend time around people who fly-fish. And the best way to meet those people is to join a fly-fishing club. Most major cities, as well as some small towns, have fly-fishing clubs. Often, the local clubs are affiliated with a larger organization such as the Federation of Fly-Fishers, Trout Unlimited, or the Smallmouth Alliance. You can find clubs by inquiring at tackle stores that sell fly-fishing gear.

Attend a meeting and you'll find an eclectic collection of like-minded souls. Usually, fly-fishing clubs meet more frequently in the winter than during the summer. A typical meeting features a speaker, perhaps a biologist or a fishing expert, and a short business session. You'll have plenty of time to meet other members and talk about fishing.

Your fellow fly-fishers can teach you all sorts of things. A club brings together anglers with varied fishing interests and abilities. You'll meet fly-tiers, rod builders, and world travelers. You may even be invited along on a fishing trip. Clubs usually devote their volunteer energy toward conservation projects and the equally important task of educating the public about fly-fishing. You can learn the fine points of the sport at club-sponsored casting clinics or fly-tying seminars. And you'll have fun, too.

motions. Don't rush the forward cast. Instead turn your head and watch the backcast unfurl behind you. Then make your forward cast.

Another problem plaguing beginners is that their fly rod goes from a nine o'clock to a three o'clock position and back on each cast. The line doesn't respond, so they speed up. They flail until frustrated, but never complete the cast. I tell new casters to try to keep the rod between eleven o'clock and one o'clock. This is an exaggeratedly tight casting sequence, but it forces the newcomer to be conscious of keeping the rod tip high. Recently, I read an expert's advice to imagine your fly rod as a paint brush and to try to paint the longest stroke possible on the ceiling. I tried it, and immediately noticed an improvement in my casting. Other experts will tell you to forget about the clock and just cast. That's good advice, too.

As a kid, I learned to fly-cast by fishing, which had advantages and shortcomings. In the tight corners of trout streams I learned to cast accurately, but I was by no means a polished caster. Some of my fishing partners—dyed-in-the-wool fly-fishermen—are atrocious casters, but they catch fish. The point is that you don't have to be a champion caster to have fun with a fly rod. All

you must do is cast well enough to get the job done. Still, you should always aspire to skillful casting. A good caster gets more pleasure out of fly-fishing.

Flies

Flies imitate the insects, minnows, and other critters that fish eat. Flies are categorized as dry flies, wet flies, nymphs, streamers, and bucktails. Some flies primarily used for bass and pike are called bugs or poppers. A few flies, including some found in this book, defy categorization and are best called critters. Dry flies imitate mayflies and other insects floating on the surface. Wet flies and nymphs represent aquatic insects. Streamers and bucktails look like minnows and small fish. Critters look like critters.

Dry Fly

Each fly style calls for different fishing techniques. Dry flies are frequently used by stream trout anglers, who cast upstream and allow the fly to float naturally with the current. Wet flies are usually cast across and fished downstream. When the wet fly reaches the apex of its drift, it swings across the current. Nymphs can be fished upstream or down. Anglers sometimes drift them naturally and other times retrieve them to create a swimming motion. Streamers and bucktails are fished with quick jerks that imitate the darting action of a minnow. Bugs and poppers are chugged across the surface like a swimming frog or mouse.

Wet Fly

My fly boxes contain dozens of flies. Most I've tied myself, but some were given to me by friends or chance acquaintances I met while fishing. Some flies trigger fine memories—a fly box is a personal thing. The best way to begin a fly collection is with a book like this one. Get the flies recommended for the type of fishing you want to do. You can buy flies through catalogs and at sport

Streamer

shops. Beware of cheap flies; they may be poorly tied. Buy the best flies you can afford from an established fly-fishing outlet. It's a good idea to buy at least two of each pattern. Then, if you lose a fly that's catching fish, you'll have another one along.

Fly boxes come in a wide range of prices and styles. The most important features on any fly box are a tight latch and sturdy hinges. Foam-lined boxes are the most versatile. Boxes with separate compartments are best for dry flies. Metal clips and fleece are best for wets, nymphs, streamers, and bucktails. Choose fly boxes that are small enough to fit comfortably in the pockets of your fly-fishing vest or other storage compartments.

Fly box

Flies can be cared for with minimal maintenance. Rust is your worst enemy. Dry out your flies thoroughly after use and make sure you dry out the interior of your fly box if it gets wet. Sometimes flies get matted and bedraggled in storage or from catching fish. Heat up a teapot and hold the fly in the steam with a hemostat to restore its shape.

Other stuff

Advertisers and outdoor writers always try to convince fly-fishers that they can't catch fish without enough gear, gadgets, and paraphernalia to sink a canoe. I've tried to take a Spartan approach, with marginal success. At some point you'll need to purchase a fly vest to store your fly boxes, leader tippets, line snips, and the like. You'll also find waders, and perhaps a float tube, awfully handy. Maybe you'll even spring for a special fishing hat. Whether you actually need four fly rods, ten fly lines, reels and extra spools, special clothing, fly-fishing art, and all the other stuff you see in stores and catalogs is a personal matter. Right now, I'm trying to rationalize another fly rod, but first I have to replace my leaky waders . . .

As with any outdoor sport, the gear game is endless. Play it to please yourself and become a better angler. Just don't let all that pricey paraphernalia scare you away from taking up the sport. You don't have to spend a fortune to have fun with a fly rod.

Willow creel

From the Dock

Bluegills and other panfish

Most north-woods fly-fishing careers begin at the end of a dock. New fly rod in hand, the beginner invariably heads to the nearest dock (you're never far from a dock in the north country) and hopes no one is watching. Like a baby bird learning to fly, the beginner flaps and flails. Then magic happens. Somehow, amid the tangles and other troubles, a pint-sized sunfish takes the fly, transforming the clumsy new fly rod into a quivering wand. The sunnie is landed, admired, and released. And fly-fishing gains another new recruit.

Some fly-fishers, especially summer-cabin owners, never go beyond the dock. Their fly-fishing is limited to occasional relaxing evenings spent casting tiny cork poppers to the ever hungry small sunfish that inhabit shoreline shallows within casting range of the dock. These casual casters lack snob appeal, but they have fun.

If you want to catch bigger bluegills on flies, you need a more serious approach. Large bluegills are surprisingly finicky and elusive. The best time to fish for them is during the early summer spawn, when they are concentrated in the shallows. Male

Some fly-fishers never go beyond the dock, but they still have lots of fun.

Bluegill

bluegills strike at flies to defend their nest and females continue to feed while spawning.

In the north country, the bluegill spawn takes place from late May through June and into July. The spawning activity peaks when the water temperature reaches 69 degrees. Generally, dark, bog-stained lakes warm up before clear waters. Look for bluegill nests—circular depressions a foot or two in diameter in the lake bottom—in water less than four feet deep. You may see the male bluegills guarding their nests.

Bluegills are most active early and late in the day. A few years ago, outdoor writer Mike Furtman took me to his secret bluegill honeyhole, a tiny lake in northwestern Wisconsin. The first afternoon, we worked the shoreline from canoes, casting small cork poppers and foam spiders. The fishing was frustrating. We caught runt largemouth bass and silver-dollar sunnies, but the big bluegills eluded us.

Bluegill conservation

Fishing for bluegills has deteriorated on many north-country lakes, often to a much greater degree than fishing for popular game fish like bass and walleyes. Typically, small panfish remain abundant in the lake, but larger ones disappear. Anglers say the panfish are stunted because of overpopulation. But it's more likely the sunnies are overfished. Anglers let the little ones go and keep the big ones; eventually, the lake's bluegill population consists mostly of small fish. The "keepers" are continually cropped off by anglers willing to settle for smaller and smaller sunfish.

Fish managers are looking for ways to restore large bluegills in lakes where they were once abundant, often by setting restrictive bag limits to reduce the harvest. Anglers can do their part by practicing catch-and-release. Keep some medium-sized bluegills for dinner and throw back the bigger ones. Then you or someone else can catch them again.

Mike and his wife, Mary Jo, finally located them just before dark, when the husky sunfish moved in to feed along the edges of aquatic weedbeds on the shallow end of the lake. We first caught them by slowly retrieving small, drab nymphs and wet flies a few inches beneath the surface. As darkness approached, we started catching them on the surface. Foam spiders proved more effective than cork poppers. The next morning, we found bluegills in the shoreline shallows at dawn, but they retreated to the depths when the sun climbed higher.

The bluegills in this small lake seemed to follow a familiar and predictable north-country fishing pattern: they were most active and accessible to fly-fishers during the dim hours of dawn and dusk. At midday, the sunlit shallows are a harsh environment where fish and their prey are vulnerable to birds and other predators. At twilight, the shadowed shallows are more inviting. Sunfish and other predators leave their deepwater haunts and move to shallow areas to feed. And the savvy fly-fisher waits there for them.

Tackle and techniques

The perfect sunfish fly rod is light and supple, with enough backbone to throw a #10 cork popper. Most 4-weight and 5-weight models fill the bill. A weight-forward floating line will handle foam bugs and poppers, but an intermediate line makes it easier to detect delicate strikes when fishing with wet flies and nymphs. Try fishing along the edge of weedbeds with a sinking line during the day. In most situations, a 7 1/2-foot leader with a 4X tippet should suffice.

Stock your fly box with cork poppers, foam bugs, wet flies, and nymphs. Don't worry about imitating specific insects (except during a heavy hatch) or other critters. Vary your fly and popper selection by size, shape, and color. For instance, yellow, black, and white are effective colors for cork poppers. Carry poppers in each of these colors in various sizes. Many anglers prefer concave-faced poppers because they make an attractive gurgling pop when twitched across the surface. Traditional wet flies like the Black Gnat, McGinty, or Wooly Worm, less than one inch in length, are time-honored subsurface patterns. Easy-to-tie nymphs like the Muskrat or Hare's Ear work, too.

Base your fly-fishing technique on common sense. If waves ripple the surface, fish with wet flies and nymphs. When the surface is still, try fishing with poppers or foam bugs. Bluegills seem to prefer a slow, twitching retrieve. Often they'll hover near a fly and inspect it before striking. Set the hook immediately when you see or feel a strike, because bluegills will spit out an artificial fly just as quickly as they inhale it.

Panfish bug and poppers

If the bluegills seem finicky or you are unsure which fishing method is most productive, try fishing with a popper and a "dropper" nymph. Tie a cork popper to your tippet. Then attach a small nymph—about #14—to a twelve- to eighteen-inch segment of two-pound tippet material. Tie this dropper to the hook bend on the popper. As you fish, the nymph will trail beneath the popper and probably attract the most strikes. The floating popper acts as a strike indicator, twitching or dipping beneath the surface when a bluegill takes the nymph.

Crappies

Although few fly-fishers pursue them, crappies can be taken with flies during the spring spawn. Crappies spawn along shorelines when the water warms to 62 degrees. Look for areas with a hard bottom. Crappies are especially attracted to fallen trees and other cover. On many lakes, local anglers know well the prime spawning areas. If you see boats or shore anglers clustered in one location, probably crappies are nearby.

Crappie

What to cast? How about a $1/32$-ounce marabou crappie jig? You can buy inexpensive crappie jigs at most sport shops. Start out with a 6-weight rod matched with a weight-forward, floating fly line and a nine-foot leader tapered to 4X. Cast out, allow a few seconds for the jig to sink, and then begin your retrieve. You should be able to fish your jig at least three feet beneath the surface. If the crappies are deeper, try a sink-tip or sinking fly line. Fan cast to cover the area, making sure you fish close to submerged trees, boulders, and other cover. Crappies are willing biters, but you may need to present the fly within inches of the fish to elicit a strike. Crappies travel in schools, so where you catch one, you should find more.

In the summer, crappies suspend in deep water. But in the evening, the crappie schools may move toward the surface or into the shallows to feed. You can catch them with jigs, sinking flies, cork poppers, or even dry flies. Usually the best fishing is at sunset. Don't be surprised if you land a bass, or even an errant walleye, when fishing for twilight crappies.

No respect

Rock bass and yellow perch, common in northern lakes, readily take flies, but few fly-fishers are happy to catch them. Most anglers consider rock bass a shabby cousin to the smallmouth, and undersized but hungry perch pose an angling nuisance. But piscatorial virtues are in the eye of the beholder. Delicious yellow perch are prized around the lower

Great Lakes. In clear Ozark streams, anglers enjoy catching rock bass, which they call goggle-eyes. Maybe north-woods anglers are missing out on something.

Bold and Brash

Smallmouth and largemouth bass

"I like it best when it's humid and 90 degrees," said Greg Breining. "It can be as steamy as a Turkish bath, and I don't mind."

Those rainy-day musings of a smallmouth bass fisherman came as we floated an eight-mile stretch of the upper Mississippi River. A steady rain had begun just minutes before we launched the canoe, and it showed no sign of letting up. For a fly-fisher like Breining, the stable weather associated with a heat wave means the smallmouth will be active and eager to take popping bugs. Unstable, rainy weather usually translates into slower fishing.

We got wet, but we caught bass by working flies in the eddies and slack water along the shoreline. Breining, who is exceptionally adept with a fly rod and a canoe paddle, sat in the stern, guiding the canoe and casting a sinking fly of his own design called the Chimpanzee. The fly, essentially an imitation of a jig-and-pig (a heavy jig tipped with pork rind that is a popular bass bait), is an unruly concoction of marabou, deer hair, and rubber legs tied on a jig hook. A split shot is crimped and epoxied to the hook for weight. The

In lightly fished wilderness lakes, bass grow fat and sassy.

Chimpanzee

Chimpanzee is ugly and nontraditional, but functional. It sinks like a rock and—to a bass—looks good to eat.

We drifted downstream with the current. The trick to catching smallmouth, Breining says, is recognizing the places where they live. Unlike trout, which hold in the current, river smallmouth prefer quiet water. The heads of shoreline eddies always offer good places to try, as do slack areas with a rocky bottom or woody cover. Breining advised casting my balsa popper into likely spots, then giving it a couple of gurgling pops. If nothing struck within a few seconds, he said to pick up and cast again.

Forget about trout techniques

Fly-fishing guide Tim Holschlag says trout anglers have a tough time with stream smallmouths. First, they have trouble casting the air-resistant flies and bugs used for bass. And then they fish in all the wrong places. In order to catch bass, trouters must hone their river-reading skills.

"Smallmouth bass in rivers are even harder to catch than trout," he says.

Whether or not bassing poses more challenge than trout fishing is open to debate, but certainly these fish species behave differently in streams. Trout are current-oriented and smallmouth bass are not. Turned loose on a smallmouth bass stream, a trouter will fish the current, where trout feed. But you'll find few bass in the current. To catch smallmouths, look for quiet water and cover such as logs or rocks.

Holschlag says trouters often use inappropriate flies. The essence of trout fishing is imitating the natural prey that the trout eat; not so with smallmouths. When fishing for river bass, don't try to match the hatch. Bass are attracted more to a fly's behavior than its appearance. The best smallmouth patterns gurgle and undulate. Most are about two to four inches long. Although they are more air-resistant than tiny trout patterns, Holschlag says effective smallmouth flies can be cast with a 7-weight or lighter rod.

"When you fly-fish, you look for active fish," he said. "On the other hand, bait fishermen can anchor and thoroughly work a spot."

Breining occasionally anchors to fish a promising spot, but because he uses a canoe, he rarely paddles back upstream to work through another portion of the pool or fish the far bank. Instead he "reads" the river ahead as he drifts downstream, and fishes the most promising bank. Usually this means staying on the outside bend, where the water along shore is deeper.

River bassing is best when the water reaches low summertime levels. Water temperatures warm up and the bass are most active. On a large, turbid stream like the upper Mississippi, the water clarity improves. Generally, the bass are easier to locate in low water, although Breining has had outstanding fishing by working the banks when the Mississippi was rolling hard with runoff. He theorizes that the slack water along the banks offers one of the few places where smallmouth can escape the current when the water is high.

Although Breining usually fishes from a canoe, his friend Tim Holschlag prefers to use a johnboat. These stable flat-bottomed boats have a shallow draft, which means they'll float through shallow riffles where a typical V-hulled boat would run aground. Although Holschlag prefers to row his boat with oars, you can power a johnboat with a small outboard or an electric motor.

Smallmouth streams

You can find stream smallmouth in habitat ranging from large rivers like the Mississippi and St. Croix to tiny creeks. Generally speaking, smallmouth prefer rocky-bottomed streams that become too warm during the summer to support trout. Many medium-sized north-country rivers meet this definition, and many are lightly fished. Fly-fishers willing to explore the streams in their bailiwick can find superb fishing.

What makes a good smallmouth stream? Habitat is the key. The best streams have hard, rocky bottoms and support an abundance of crayfish and minnows. Slow-moving marshy streams are great places to fish for pike or hunt ducks, but support few smallmouths. Also, the bass must have access to deepwater wintering areas. Studies in Wisconsin have found that smallmouth make autumn migrations of twenty miles or more to reach deep pools where they spend the winter in a dormant state.

Another factor to consider is fishing pressure. North-woods smallmouth are slow growing and easy to catch with bait or artificials. Streams and lakes frequently fished by catch-and-keep anglers are often populated with numerous runt bass. On creeks and small rivers, the available habitat may support only a small population of good-sized bass. Taking home a limit of keepers can put a serious dent in the local bass population. Practice catch-and-release.

Tackle and techniques

You don't need special tackle to fly-fish for smallmouths. In most situations, you can get by with a 6- or 7-weight rod matched with a floating weight-forward line. More important than having the right tackle is knowing how to use it. The typical fly-fisher used to fishing for trout in small streams may not have the fly-casting skills necessary to accurately cast a bulky bass fly fifty feet or more. As a rule, the bass anglers I know are considerably better fly-casters than most of my trout-fishing friends. Smallmouth guides say they

Strike indicators

A strike indicator is simply a bobber for fly-fishing. Although strike indicators come in several styles, all are essentially the same thing: a small, brightly colored floating object that attaches to your leader. When you get a strike, the indicator twitches or dips beneath the surface—just like a bobber.

Strike indicators help detect strikes when you are fishing with subsurface flies. They are most helpful when you are casting upstream and retrieving a fly with the current. In this situation, a smallmouth can inhale and exhale a fly so quickly that you won't feel the strike. If you attach a strike indicator to your leader, you'll detect subtle strikes.

often begin their fishing sessions with an impromptu casting lesson.

Next, you must know how to work a fly to create a bass-attracting action. The dead-drift methods used to fish dry flies and nymphs for trout aren't very effective for smallmouth. You have to make the fly behave like something that's good to eat. A floating bug should wiggle and twitch like a frog, while sinking patterns should scuttle across the bottom like a crayfish or some other critter.

Novices often try to impart action to their flies by moving the rod, as you would do when fishing with spinning gear. This doesn't work with fly tackle. The resistance of the fly line on the water causes a flexible fly rod to bend. In order to move the fly with the rod, you need to make such a sweeping action that the rod ends up in an awkward position for setting the hook when you get a strike. The proper way to make most fly retrieves is to point the rod at the water and to strip in the line with your hand. You can change the retrieve by varying the stripping action. With this method, you won't have slack in the line. To set the hook, just lift the rod upward by cocking your wrist.

Smallmouth in lakes

Minnesota's Boundary Waters Canoe Area Wilderness, Ontario's Quetico Provincial Park, Wisconsin's Chequamegon Bay on Lake Superior, and Michigan's Sylvania Wilderness Area all offer outstanding fly-fishing for smallmouth bass. Go to any of these places at the right time of year and you can expect to catch bruiser bass weighing four to six pounds. Few other smallmouth fishing areas anywhere in North America can make a similar boast.

Surprisingly, you can fish these places during the prime portion of the fishing season and not

Stripping line

see other fly-fishers. In fact, you may not encounter anyone fishing for bass. With the exception of Chequamegon Bay, these waters lie in remote wilderness areas accessible mostly by canoe. Few anglers are willing to paddle and portage to go fishing. And most wilderness anglers prefer to fish for walleyes, northern pike, or lake trout. As a result, the lightly fished wilderness smallmouths have the opportunity to grow fat and sassy.

Every summer, I make at least one day trip into East Pike Lake on the eastern edge of the Boundary Waters Canoe Area Wilderness. I have a simple fishing strategy: If the lake is calm, I cast small cork poppers along the rocky shorelines. If waves stir the surface, I fish the same areas with weighted Wooly Buggers. The smallmouth I fool rarely top two pounds, but the fishing action is consistent. If East Pike were deeper into the wilderness, perhaps I'd catch bigger fish.

Someday, I'm going fishing with Roger LaPenter on Lake Superior's Chequamegon Bay so I can do just that. The bay is one of the few easily accessible waters with a healthy population of hefty smallmouths. LaPenter is a fly-fishing guide based in Ashland, Wisconsin, who chases the bay's smallmouth whenever the wind and weather allow him to do so. Chequamegon, a large, shallow bay, provides smallmouth habitat rarely found throughout Superior's cold expanse. The best time to fish for them with flies is during May, June, and July. Often you can catch bass on the surface with popping bugs.

LaPenter recommends using hard-bodied poppers or sliders made of cork or closed-cell foam in hook sizes #6 and #4. A wide-mouthed popper makes a popping sound as you pull it across the surface, while a bullet-shaped slider dives a few inches deep when you pull it and then floats back to the surface. He prefers hard-bodied poppers, because the smallmouths often swallow deer hair bugs and are difficult to unhook and release. He also uses barbless hooks to lessen the chances of injuring fish.

You don't need heavy gear to fish the bay. LaPenter prefers 6- and 7-weight rods, and says you can get by with a 5-weight if it isn't too windy. He uses a weight-forward floating line and a leader tapering to 10-pound-test. The heavy tippet helps free your fly if you get hung up.

Surface fishing is easy. LaPenter offers time-honored advice: Cast out your popper and then wait for the wake of tiny rings to subside. Bay bass strike most often when the popper is sitting still. After the rings subside, make a quick strip of the line so the popper gurgles across the surface, and then wait again. If you're lucky, the popper will disappear in a violent swirl.

Where and when

Smallmouth are easy to find in north-woods lakes. Just look for rocks and wood. Fallen trees, boulders, and rubble provide places where smallmouth can hide and ambush their prey. Rocky points, boulder-strewn bays, moderately shallow shorelines, islands, and reefs are all good places to look for smallmouth. Although they are most accessible to fly-fishers in water less than six feet deep, you can investigate deeper water using a full-sinking line with leech or minnow imitations.

Smallmouth shift locations according to the season. In the spring, they are lethargic in the cold water and difficult to catch by any fishing method. As the water warms to 60 degrees, usually during June, the bass move to rocky shoreline areas to spawn. Like largemouth bass and bluegills, they are nest builders that will strike at anything that comes near their nest. Some of the largest bass of the season—spawn-heavy females—are taken at this time. Following the spawn, smallmouth retreat to deeper water to recover and are again difficult to catch for a couple of weeks. They become more active as the water temperature reaches 70 degrees, and provide good fishing, especially at dawn and dusk, during the traditional angling dog days of July and August. As the water temperatures cool in September, the smallmouth move toward deepwater wintering areas.

Smallmouth flies

To Minneapolis guide Tim Holschlag, an effective smallmouth fly has more than just a pretty face. Too many bass flies, he says, are tied to fool the angler instead of the fish. For a fly pattern to find a place in his fly box, it must be versatile enough to work in many angling situations, durable enough to catch a couple of dozen smallmouth, simple to tie, and easy to cast.

Bass flies are designed to create a disturbance. Poppers and sliders put up a fuss on the surface when you retrieve them. And Greg Breining says subsurface flies like his Chimpanzee pattern "move water" as they hop along the bottom. What are the best colors? In clear waters, use flies that are dark, drab and ugly. Olive, brown, and black fill the bill. Bright colors such as yellow, white, and chartreuse are more visible in stained waters, but will fool bass in clear waters, too.

With these criteria in mind, it's easy to come up with a short list of flies that will consistently

Top or bottom?

Most bass patterns are either popping bugs that are fished on the surface or jig-like flies that are hopped across the bottom. Smallmouths most frequently forage on crayfish and minnows near the bottom, although they'll readily rise to the surface in shallow water. Even though you'll lose an occasional fly, keep your subsurface presentations close to the bottom. That's where the bass are.

catch smallmouth bass in lakes and streams. For subsurface flies, use heavily weighted patterns such as the Chimpanzee, the Rabbit Strip Leech, the Clouser Minnow, and the Wooly Bugger. Holschlag ties a rubber-legged Wooly Bugger he calls the Holschlag Hackle Fly that is a good crayfish imitation. All of these patterns can be weighted with dumbbell eyes so they sink quickly and hop along the bottom when retrieved.

Popping bugs come in a variety of styles. Perhaps the most ingenious is the Dahlberg Diver, a pattern designed on the St. Croix River that's gained nationwide popularity in recent years. The Dahlberg Diver has a flat bottom and a sloping clipped deer hair head that meets a stiff deer hair collar. When you pull the fly, it dives and swims

The Dahlberg Diver

Pro fly-fisher Larry Dahlberg of Brainerd, Minnesota, says that fly-rodders fall into two categories: those who fish for trout and those who fish for predator fish. Trouters try to tie flies that look like the mayflies and other life-forms eaten by their quarry. In streams, most trout flies are dead-drifted in the current. On the other hand, an angler after predatory species must convince the fish that the fly is alive. The action of the fly is more important than exact imitation of the prey species. The Dahlberg Diver falls into the second category. When you retrieve the fly with sharp tugs, it dives a few inches beneath the surface, swims a short distance and then surfaces. It's an action few game fish can resist.

Larry developed the fly nearly thirty years ago to catch a certain finicky bass in a northern Wisconsin lake. At the time, he was guiding anglers on the upper St. Croix River and he discovered the diving fly was dynamite for smallmouths. Gradually, the fly grew famous. It's now a popular bass bug. Dahlberg has used his divers, tied in different sizes and colors, to catch a variety of fish species in locations from the tropics to the Arctic.

Carl's beautiful bugs

When Carl Bradley gives you one of his deer hair bugs, you don't want to fish with it. A New York fly-tier who likes to fish the trout streams of northwestern Wisconsin, Carl ties wonderful popping bugs with exquisite spots and stripes. In addition to standard poppers and frogs, he also creates perch and sunfish from deer hair.

The secret to tying good poppers, he says, is tightly packing small bunches of deer hair to build a dense, water-resistant body.

beneath the surface with enticing motion. You can fish it with a sinking line as an imitation crankbait.

Although popping bugs made from clipped deer hair have homespun character, smallmouth guides Holschlag and LaPenter both prefer poppers made from cork or dense closed-cell foam. If you purchase poppers, choose sturdy, well-built models, because they float better and last longer. Carry several styles, colors, and sizes. Sometimes the bass want a bold popping action. Other times they prefer a more subtle approach.

Largemouth bass

Largemouth bass are the most popular game fish in North America—except in the north woods. Even though hundreds of lakes offer excellent bass fishing, a minority of fly-fishers pursue large-mouths. And the majority miss out on lots of fun.

"Largemouth bass provide consistent fishing," says Ashland, Wisconsin, fly-fishing guide Roger LaPenter. "About the only time it slows down is when there's a drastic drop in the barometric pressure."

LaPenter prefers to fish for bass on the surface, using floating poppers and sliders. He fishes with both deer hair and hard-bodied (cork, balsa, and foam) bugs. On the lakes that he fishes, he rarely resorts to subsurface patterns.

"The thrill in catching largemouths is taking them on the surface," he says.

LaPenter has an easy method for finding bass lakes, which will work wherever they're located in the north country. He opens an area map and looks for small, out of the way lakes. Nearly all contain largemouths, and many are lightly fished. When scouting a new area, use this method to come up with a list of potential lakes. Then call the area's natural resources office and ask for some information about the lakes on your list. When you hang up, your list should be narrowed to a few good lakes.

Be sure to ask about access to the lakes. Some are accessible with a boat, but others are best fished with a float tube. If no public land abuts the lake, you may need permission to cross private property. Surprisingly, some of the best largemouth lakes are small, private waters ringed with cabins. Inaccessible to the public, these lakes receive light fishing pressure.

LaPenter offers simple fishing advice: Get out past the weeds and cast back toward shore. Look for fish to be holding near aquatic vegetation or shoreline cover. In these small lakes, many bass remain near shore throughout the summer. A good strategy is to fish along the edge of the weed line. When a largemouth strikes, wait a second or two before you set the hook. Keep steady pressure on the fish. If the bass burrows into the weeds, go to the fish and dig it out.

Bass bugs are wind resistant and difficult to cast with light tackle. A 7- to 9-weight fly rod matched with a weight-forward line will work the best. Use a 7 1/2-foot leader tapered to a 0X or 10-pound tippet. If you have trouble getting the leader to straighten out when you cast, cut it back even shorter.

What flies? Try hair bugs that imitate frogs or mice. Hard poppers from two to four inches long will catch fish, too. You can vary the gurgles and pops in your retrieve, but often you'll find these backwoods bass aren't choosy. If surface action is slow, try fishing subsurface leech patterns like the Wooly Bugger or large streamers like the Lefty's Deceiver or the Muddler Minnow. LaPenter said he occasionally finds active bass holding along the

Don't jump the gun

In some places the largemouth bass season is closed during the spring to protect fish spawning in shallow water. Unfortunately, this is one of the best times to catch big bass. Like bluegills, largemouths will strike at any fly that passes near their nest. Some anglers fish for spawning bass during the closed season, rationalizing their actions by practicing catch-and-release. Don't join them. Catch-and-release, like ignorance, is no excuse to break the law.

edge of a deep drop-off. He goes after them with a sinking line and a Clouser Minnow. The method is effective, he says, but less exciting than catching largemouths on the surface.

Up a Creek

Brook, brown, and rainbow trout

The sun hung low and the mosquitoes were friendly when I waded into the upper end of the beaver pond. My fishing time was limited, so I planned to reel up and leave before darkness fell —highly unusual behavior for this fly-fisherman.

The pond was still but no fish were rising, so I started casting a #8 Opossum Nymph in the current where the stream entered the pond. Nothing stirred, so I switched to a #14 Professor and promptly lost it by overreacting to a savage strike. Unfortunately, it was the only Professor in the fly box. The closest pattern was a #16 Tellico Nymph, which has a yellow floss body like the Professor.

Apparently, the yellow body was the ticket, because the brookies went after the Tellico with vicious enthusiasm. The first one was a plump eleven-incher, followed by a pair of fourteen-inchers. I moved along the edge of the pond, casting to the moving current near the center. The next fish stopped the fly and started taking line when I set the hook. This brook trout meant business. We battled for five minutes, until the heavy sixteen-incher was finning in the water beside me. The fish's flanks showed the vivid palette of colors

Only those who fish for brook trout know its vivid palette of colors.

known only to those who fish for brook trout. That palette belonged in the pond and not in a frying pan. Carefully, I reached for the fly so I could slide the hook from the trout without touching it. But the big brookie thrashed and broke the tippet, disappearing with my only Tellico Nymph. It was time to leave. Surprising even myself, I reeled up and hiked out to the truck.

Most fly-fishers aren't likely to tell you the whereabouts of their favorite places, but you can find trout fishing like this in small, cold streams throughout the north woods. In northern Wisconsin, your quarry will probably be fat brown trout, while in the wilds of Ontario you can find

All about mayflies

Most dry flies, nymphs, and emergers imitate different mayfly species at the various stages in their life cycle. The mayfly is a common trout stream insect, although their abundance and importance to trout varies in north-woods streams. The fertile, spring-fed rivers of northern Wisconsin have prolific mayfly populations, but mayflies are less common in the rocky rivers of the Canadian Shield. The delicate flies are also found in most northern lakes.

The mayfly life cycle begins when tiny nymphs hatch from eggs deposited in the water by adult mayflies. Mayfly nymphs of various species live in a variety of aquatic habitats, but they share one prerequisite: unpolluted water. Some species burrow in the silt, others cling to the underside of rocks, and some swim about on the stream bottom. Feeding on algae and organic matter, the nymphs grow to maturity in one year. Then, at about the same time as their parents the year before, they emerge from the stream as adult mayflies.

This emergence is what fly-fishers call a hatch. Each mayfly species hatches at a specific time of year and usually at a specific time of day, in response to water temperature and daylight. The nymphs become active prior to the hatch, moving about on the stream bottom and in the current. Trout may remote streams with hefty hook-jawed brook trout. At times, you can find trout fishing that will rival the more famous Rocky Mountain waters.

The greatest difference is that fly-fishing in the Rockies is more consistent. Most northern streams, especially those on the Canadian Shield, are infertile and support minimal insect life. As a result, the hatches are infrequent and sporadic. Because these streams are usually fed by runoff, water levels and stream temperatures fluctuate. A stream that looks perfect in June might be nearly dry in August. This means that much of the stream is inhospitable to the fish. In order to survive, the trout concentrate wherever they find cold, deep

feed heavily on them at this time. The nymphs then rise to the surface, where they shed their nymphal husk and emerge as graceful winged adults that anglers call duns. Some mayflies flutter off immediately, while others ride the currents for a few moments while their wings dry.

The adult mayfly has a short life—lasting anywhere from a couple of hours to one day. During that time, the dun will molt into a mating stage known to anglers as a spinner. On streams with abundant mayfly populations, you may see clouds of spinners hovering over the river. They mate, the females deposit their eggs in the water, and the mayflies die. Anglers call the dead mayflies, drifting spread-eagle in the surface film, spent wings.

You can learn more about the mayflies that live in your favorite streams by turning over rocks on the stream bottom to look for nymphs. Fly-fishing retailers sell small mesh nets for collecting aquatic insects. Place the net downstream from the rocks to capture any nymphs that escape in the current. In silty areas, look for tiny holes made by nymphs burrowing into the mud. Use a fly-fishing entomology book from the local library to identify the nymphs you collect. Check around. Maybe fellow fly-fishers have already researched the entomology of local waters. If your fishing locale has enough fly-fishers to support a fly shop, the proprietor can tell you when and where to look for hatches.

water. When the water is low, you may walk a half mile between fishable pools.

Spring-fed streams like the Bois Brule River in northern Wisconsin are exceptions. These streams have consistent water flows throughout the year. And because spring water maintains a constant year-round temperature, these streams run cooler in the summer and warmer in the winter than runoff rivers. Generally, spring-fed streams have abundant insect life and more trout habitat. Various mayflies and other insects hatch consistently during the summer. On a spring-fed stream, you can "match the hatch" by using a fly that imitates the natural insect the trout are eating.

On runoff streams, more often you'll "fish blind" with a fly designed to attract strikes. The trout in these streams have a limited menu, so they'll strike at anything that looks edible. Nevertheless, you'll still find that some fly patterns outperform others. One such fly is the Pass Lake, a time-honored north-country wet fly. The Pass Lake has a black chenille body and a white calf-tail wing, and this contrast seems key to the pattern's effectiveness.

Pass Lake

"The Pass Lake works where it shouldn't work," says Larry Meicher of Madison, Wisconsin, whose nickname among his fishing cronies is the Pass Lake Kid.

Meicher most frequently fishes the Pass Lake as a wet fly in sizes #14 and #16. However, he also ties Pass Lakes as dry flies and as emergers, which represent hatching insects. Regardless of what fly is hatching or what the trout are eating, he usually fishes with his trusty Pass Lake.

"I can always pick out that white wing," he said.

Many fly-fishers use a weighted #10 Pass Lake to probe for trout in pools and runs. The Pass Lake is best fished downstream in traditional wet fly style. This means you cast the fly across the stream and let it swim with the current. As the fly moves downstream from you, it will start to swing across the current. This is when you can expect the fish to strike.

The Muddler Minnow is another fly that will rouse trout from their lairs. Originated on the storied brook trout waters of Ontario's Nipigon River, the Muddler imitates the sculpin, a common baitfish in many trout streams. The fly has a bulky head of clipped deer hair that creates a distinctive sculpinlike silhouette. Like many productive flies, the Muddler is effective in a variety of circumstances. You can fish a weighted Muddler along the bottom as a streamer or float an unweighted pattern on the surface to imitate a grasshopper.

Sparse Muddler Minnow

Wet or dry versatility is the trademark of the Arrowhead, another fly that originated in the north woods. The Arrowhead is a simple hackle fly that doesn't seem to represent anything in particular, but the trout think it looks good to eat. The Arrowhead floats well, but you can pull it beneath the surface and fish it wet. Some Brule River guides say the Arrowhead is effective throughout the fishing season.

What other flies should a stream trout angler's fly box contain? No two fly-fishers would have the same answer for that question. And most carry more than one fly box. But trouters are creatures of habit and tradition. Although they most often fish with one or two favorite flies, they undoubtedly carry an arsenal of patterns.

Rummage through a typical trouter's collection of flies and you'll find standard dry flies like the Adams, Blue-Winged Olive, Elk Hair Caddis, Hendrickson, Light Cahill, Quill Gordon, and

Royal Coachman in sizes #10 through #18. Favorite nymphs include the Pheasant Tail, Hare's Ear, and Zug Bug in sizes #10 through #14. Montanas, Wooly Worms, and Wooly Buggers from #4 to #10 round out the nymph selection. Or course, you'll also find Arrowheads, Pass Lakes, and Muddler Minnows and time-honored streamers like the Black-Nosed Dace and Mickey Finn.

Upstream or down?

You can go two directions on a trout stream: upstream or down. The one you choose depends upon the water level and your fishing method. Alert and wary, stream trout always face into the current. On bright days, when the water is low or when trout are holding in shallow water, they may see you and scoot for cover before you get a chance to cast. This is especially true if you are walking downstream.

As a general rule, it is best to fish upstream. Dry fly anglers nearly always fish upstream, as do many experienced nymphers. With a stealthy upstream approach, you can sneak into casting positions undetected by the trout. The exception is that wet flies and streamers are often fished downstream. These techniques are most effective during low light periods and when streams are running at normal levels. Try fishing downstream with a Pass Lake at dusk in June, not during midday in August.

Trout fishing rewards sneaky, cunning behavior. Trout can sense the vibrations from clumsy footsteps or loud voices. They'll also spook from a poor, noisy cast or an unnatural-appearing fly. Be quiet and crouch to keep a low profile, even if you're fishing upstream. When wading, try not to push a wake ahead of you. Stealth always pays off.

Best times

Magazines often picture fly-fishers standing in sun-dappled streams, but sunshine is the bane of north-country trouters. When the summer sun shines on the water, brookies and browns retreat to the dark corners of their domain. The best times to fish are dawn and dusk, when the sun is low and the fish venture out to feed. Most mayflies and other aquatic insects are active during low-light periods, especially evening.

An exception to this rule comes in early spring, when the stream water runs icy cold. Then trout are most active when the midday sun warms the water. If the water is very cold—numbing to your touch—the trout may be unwilling to take flies. Fishing with bait is more productive.

Dependable caddis

Although heavy hatches are infrequent, you'll see caddis flies fluttering erratically over trout streams throughout the fishing season. Like the mayfly, the caddis begins life at the bottom of the stream. Some caddis larvae are free-swimming, but most varieties build a protective cocoon of tiny rocks or sticks. You can find these cocoons attached to submerged rocks. The larva hatches into a fly that may live for a month or more in streamside vegetation. Caddis flies have a very different appearance from mayflies. When at rest, their wings fold in a tentlike shape over the body.

Because trout may see caddis floating on the surface just about anytime, they'll often strike caddis imitations. Try fishing with caddis dry flies when you don't see a hatch or when trout are rising sporadically. Trout will even strike at caddis flies when rising to a mayfly hatch. Flies imitating caddis pupa—the stage when caddis larva leave the stream bottom to emerge at the surface as adults—are effective at times. Allow the weighted fly to sink to the bottom, then jerk it quickly to the surface to imitate a hatching caddis.

Fly-fishing in streams is usually best from late spring until midsummer, because stream flows and water temperatures are optimum for trout. Later in the summer, water levels drop and stream temperatures start to rise. Some north-woods streams, particularly large, boulder-strewn rivers, may become too warm for trout. The rocks absorb energy from the sun, then radiate warmth into the river. When this occurs, trout seek out springs and cool feeder creeks. If you stumble across one of these cool-water refuges, you'll find an incredible concentration of trout. Practice catch-and-release, because they're vulnerable to overfishing.

As the days grow shorter and the waters cool in late summer and early fall, brook and brown trout prepare to spawn. If your favorite pools seem devoid of fish, look for gravel riffles or similar spawning areas. This is a good time to search for larger-than-average fish, because the big ones leave the shelter of their lairs to spawn. Brook trout become especially beautiful at this time of year, taking on brilliant spawning coloration.

Beaver pond beauties

Beaver activity on a trout stream can be both a blessing and a curse. Beaver dams may block fish migration, and sun-warmed beaver ponds can become too tepid for trout. But beaver dams, especially new ones, often provide the deepwater habitat necessary to grow big trout in small streams. Some beaver ponds remain productive trout waters for decades. That's why beaver ponds are synonymous with north-woods brook trout fishing.

For the fly-fisher, a beaver pond may be the only place on an otherwise brushy stream where it is possible to make a cast. And even at the pond, the alder brush will conspire against you. Beaver ponds are rarely easy to fish. If you're lucky, you may be able to fish from a float tube or canoe. More often, you'll be forced to wallow through muck and brambles just to reach the water.

Beaver pond trout are fickle critters. Shy when the sun is high, they eat an early breakfast at dawn and a late dinner at dusk. Often the trout are concentrated in limited areas that provide deep water and cover. If you find these fish, you may think you've discovered a mother lode of brook trout. In reality, you tripped across one of the few places in the stream where trout can survive. Treat it with respect.

Often, beavers build a series of ponds. Ron Shoberg, a Duluth, Minnesota, brook trout fisherman, says the uppermost pond is the one most likely to hold fish. "Sometimes the ponds downstream are sterile," he says, "because the surface water running out of the upstream pond is too warm for trout."

Patience is a virtue when fishing for beaver pond brookies. The late Upper Peninsula author John Voelker, whose pen name was Robert Traver, wrote of hoarding the cast. Too many anglers, he believed, flailed away to little avail. Continued casting on a still, quiet pond alarms the fish. Fish like a heron instead. Move quietly and deliberately. Try not to make waves or ripples as you wade—a good strategy wherever you fish. Keep false casting to a minimum and make each cast count. Often you can make only one or two casts before scaring the fish. If you make a poor cast, fish it through. Picking up and casting again is like firing a warning volley.

You'll occasionally find beaver pond brookies in the mood to rise for anything, but more often visible trout activity is minimal. You're most likely to see rising trout at dawn and dusk. Use light

Beaver pond trout are fickle critters. You'll need luck as well as skill to find and catch them.

tackle and long, fine leaders. Your fly box should include a selection of small dry flies and nymphs, as well as small streamers and leech imitations such as the Mink Strip Leech. If you enjoy dry fly fishing, try your favorite patterns even if you don't see any risers. Remember, brook trout are selective feeders. As a fly-fisher, your job is to present trout with dining opportunities until you find the one they prefer.

A Brule River calendar

Wisconsin's Bois Brule is the north country's most famous trout stream. Fly-fishers have traveled to the Brule for over a century. Because the Brule has stable spring-fed flows, aquatic insect hatches are consistent. Depending upon geographic location and stream conditions, hatches on other streams, especially in northern Wisconsin, correspond with the dependable Brule.

Damian Wilmot of South Range, Wisconsin, and Keith Behn of Proctor, Minnesota, guide fly-fishers on the Brule throughout the open-water season. What follows is their calendar to Brule River hatches. You can expect to find these same insects on other northwoods streams. Just remember, you can't set your watch by nature. A passing cold front can delay insect activity, and unseasonably warm weather might accelerate the schedule.

The Hendrickson mayfly is the first hatch

of the season. Hendricksons first appear from about April 15 to May 15, typically peaking around May 1. Sometimes the peak occurs before fishing season opens. The Hendrickson duns come off around two or three o'clock in the afternoon. You can match the hatch with a #12 or #14 Light Hendrickson.

An evening hatch of Sulphurs begins about mid-May, peaking around June 1. Expect the rise to begin at dusk. Sulphurs are small mayflies, best imitated with #16 and #18 patterns. During the Sulphur hatch, Wilmot has experienced evenings where rising trout fed viciously, but not on the mayflies. When this "mystery hatch" occurs, he's tried dry flies, nymphs, and streamers with no success.

"I don't know what they're taking," he says.

Brown Drake mayflies also hatch during the first two weeks of June, although peak activity may occur on just two or three nights. Duns appear in the evening, followed by a spinner fall that starts at dusk and continues after dark. Wilmot's favorite pattern is a #10 Hackle Spinner.

The first Hexagenia mayflies (see the next chapter) are usually seen on the Brule between the tenth and twentieth of June. The giant duns appear at dusk, and the spinner fall occurs after dark. The hatch becomes unreliable after July 4.

Hatch activity is sporadic during the month of July. The first hatches of tiny Trichorythedes mayflies (anglers call them Tricos), always at midmorning, occur at the end of the month. Behn likes to fish Tricos, because you can eat breakfast before going to the river and be back in time for lunch. Look for Tricos from 10 A.M. until noon. The hatch continues through August and September.

The trouble with Tricos is their minuscule size. Behn said this is a tough hatch for novices, because they must be adept with delicate fishing techniques. The #20 to #24 Trico imitations are tough to see on the water. Leaders are tapered to a wispy 7X or 8X. A light fly rod, such as a 4-weight, is required. Once you master Tricos, you can move on to an even tinier challenge. Blue-Winged Olive mayflies—matched with #24 to #28 flies—hatch from the end of August through September. A #28 fly, by the way, is about the size of the lead tip on a pencil.

If you don't see a hatch, try fishing with a small floating caddis pattern. Caddis flies stay around throughout the summer. Wilmot also recommended ant and beetle imitations, especially for early morning fishing. Throughout the season, he fishes with a Pheasant Tail Nymph, sizes 12 to 18. A #16 or #18 Pheasant Tail will catch trout during the Sulphur hatch.

And don't forget the mouse hatch. Some of the Brule's biggest browns are fooled by deer hair mice. Anglers canoe the river after sunset, casting mice to the banks. The action is slow, but explosive. Despite the darkness, you'll know when you get a strike.

Trout tackle

As fly-fishing guides, Keith Behn and Damian Wilmot fish with dozens of anglers each summer. Often, they must help their clients make do with less than adequate equipment.

"A lot of people have gear that's too heavy," Behn said.

In his opinion, 5- or 6-weight outfits are best for north-woods streams. It is difficult to make delicate casts with a 7-weight and inexperienced anglers may have trouble casting a light 4-weight rod. Five- and 6-weights are comfortable to cast with trout flies and have enough

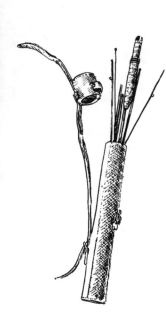

Fly rods and rod case

backbone to handle the occasional eighteen-inch or larger fish. The length of a fly rod is a matter of personal preference. Some small stream specialists prefer shorter rods—seven to eight feet—because they are easier to maneuver in brushy situations.

Most stream fishing is done with a floating line. If your typical casts are less than fifty feet, you can make precise, delicate presentations with a double-taper line. Use a weight-forward if you fish frequently with large, heavy flies, such as weighted streamers. You can use a floating line for fishing with nymphs. Add tiny nontoxic shot or similar weight to your leader to pull your nymph deeper. In deep runs or heavy currents, a sink-tip line is more efficient.

Make sure your leader matches the fishing situation. When fishing with small dry flies, use a long, fine leader—experts frequently use leaders measuring twelve feet or more in length. The long leader helps you avoid spooking rising fish with your fly line. When fishing with subsurface flies, you can use shorter leaders. Try a nine-footer for fishing with small nymphs or a leader as short as six feet for large streamers.

The size of your tippet can make the difference between catching fish and getting skunked. Generally, the size of the tippet should match the size of the fly. Dry fly anglers commonly use light 5X and 6X tippets. Although heavier and stronger tippets offer more insurance for playing and landing fish, a wary trout will refuse to strike your fly if it sees the leader. With tiny flies—#18 to #28—use 7X or 8X tippets. You can use 4X and 3X tippets for larger nymphs and streamers. An even heavier tippet is necessary when fishing for trophy brown trout at night with oversized flies.

Big flies=big trout

The biggest trout in most streams rarely are tempted by angler's flies. That's because few fly-fishers pursue big trout. From a trophy trout's perspective, eating a tiny dry fly or nymph isn't worth the effort. They prefer small fish, crayfish, and other critters that provide a substantial meal. Also, big trout occupy deep holes and sheltered places that are difficult to fish. About the only time trophy trout are vulnerable to most fly-fishers is during the Hex hatch or a similar occurrence that triggers a feeding frenzy.

Brown Trout

Although most anglers are content to fish for average trout, a few fly-fishers evolve into big trout specialists. My friend Ed Atcas of Minneapolis is one of them. He routinely catches the sort of brown trout that most anglers only dream about, often from popular trout streams. How does he do it?

The first step, he says, is learning to recognize big trout habitat. Big trout prefer deep water with rocks, logs, and other cover. A pool that produces plenty of ten-inchers won't necessarily hold a five-pounder. In fact, the deep hole where the five-pounder lives may be devoid of ten-inchers, because the big fish either eats the small trout or chases them away.

In a stream that supports brown trout, Atcas generally looks for big ones in the deeper, down-stream portions of the stream. Often, his hot spots are considered marginal trout waters. On brook trout streams, look for deep water in remote places. New beaver dams, dead-waters, and spring ponds are all possibilities. Often you'll find feeding brookies where the stream current flows into deep water.

Tactics for catching big trout differ radically from those most anglers use. First you should use huge, heavily weighted flies. Atcas likes tarpon flies, such as the Lefty's Deceiver, and nymphs the size of your little finger. He fishes the flies upstream with a fast-sinking weight-forward line. This means that his flies sink quickly to the bottom and stay there.

"Big trout rarely leave the bottom," he says. "If you want to catch them, that's where you should be fishing."

Atcas retrieves his streamers with fast strips and swims his monster nymphs along the bottom. Each likely spot gets a couple of casts, and then he moves on. Big trout often strike on the first good cast. The best strategy is to cover lots of water and put your fly in front of as many fish as you can. Atcas might wade three miles of stream in a morning's fishing. Expect to see trout follow your fly but not strike. Remember the location, and try it again some other time.

Trout stream survival

Getting there, they say, is half the fun. Stream trout fishing isn't for everyone. The best places to fish

Trophy trout tips

If a true trophy is your goal, be persistent.

- Stick with the oversized flies; they work. Leave your traditional trout flies at home so you won't be tempted to use them.
- Fish for big trout at the times they are most active: dawn, dusk, after dark, and on cloudy days.
- In waters that contain pike, walleye, or bass, look for trout near cold springs and tributaries.
- During the summer, try fishing after rains. On hot summer nights, bruiser browns can be coaxed to the surface with Dahlberg Divers or popping bugs.

are invariably a long way from anywhere else. Behn and Wilmont recently spent several days in Ontario exploring a huge river system for trophy brook trout. Every day they'd get as close to the river as they could with a vehicle and then strike off on foot. One day they walked for three hours, only to encounter a fisherman in a boat. How did he get there, they asked. He told them you could drive to the river and launch a boat just a short distance upstream. So it goes when you're exploring unfamiliar country. Undaunted by their lack of success, the pair are already planning a return trip.

"We didn't find any big brookies, but we've figured out where they are," said the ever optimistic Behn. "It's the only place on the river we didn't check out."

Both anglers know from experience that their legwork will eventually pay off with some exceptional fishing. And once they hit pay dirt, they'll set off in search of new hot spots. Brook trout anglers are like that. The water is always bluer in the next beaver pond. You have to brave bugs, bogs, and bull moose to find good fishing.

Look out for trout

A meal of fresh brook trout is a gift of the north woods. Unfortunately, brook trout taste too good for their own good. Because most anglers keep and eat the fish they catch, the quality of brook trout fishing has declined in streams and lakes you can reach by road.

Brook trout are short lived and slow growing, so it is easy to "fish out" the larger fish in a stream or lake. It would be best for brookies if anglers curbed their appetite. Release your large brookies and keep some smaller ones for a meal. Don't fill the freezer or feed the neighborhood with brook trout. Conservation is the key to better fishing. And it begins with you.

Brook trout expeditions often begin with a rumor. Trouters will believe any tale, no matter how tall, if the story somehow includes a beaver pond chock-full of fourteen-inch brook trout. The further from civilization, the better. The trouter will repeat the rumor to a fellow fly-fisher, and soon the two of them will be searching topographic maps for the mythical honeyhole and planning a fishing trip.

Occasionally, these excursions pan out. But regardless of the outcome, you can plan on putting some wear and tear on yourself and your gear. You'll be a better bushwhacker with advance preparation. Travel light. Do you need a pair of waders or can you wade wet? Will a pocket-sized fly box and some leader material suffice for tackle? Break down your fly rod and carry it in a cloth case, or secure each end with wire twist ties to better negotiate the brush. If you do bring waders, consider carrying them and putting them on at the stream. Be sure to bring food and water, a compass, insect repellant, waterproof matches, a flashlight, and two sets of keys for the vehicle. Plan ahead, and your highly anticipated expedition is far less likely to become an aborted mission.

Elegant Giants

Fishing the Hexagenia hatch

It's midsummer in northwestern Wisconsin. Daytime highs reach the eighties and thunderheads rumble across the afternoon sky, threatening to rain out the evening. Listening to reports of a nearby tornado touchdown, we fret about the weather over dinner. Despite the gloomy sky, we go fishing. Just before sundown, we slog into the swamp, armed with flashlights, fly rods, and bug dope. At the river we wish each other luck and separate to stake out promising holes and alder-canopied bends.

My spot is a sweeping turn where a spring creek enters the river. Just downstream in a tangle of brush and logs, big brown trout can hide while basking in the tributary's cool flow. Above the bend is another promising hole. Now, however, no trout are rising. Accompanied by swarming mosquitoes, I make a few casts to learn the nuances of the current before darkness falls. It's possible to work about thirty feet of line without getting hung up in the alders.

The first trout appears about the same time a nearby whippoorwill announces that night has come. A giant mayfly—fully two inches long—

The Hex hatch triggers a feeding frenzy which excites trouters as much as it does trout.

floats downstream on the smooth currents and disappears in a noisy swirl. Scientists call this bug the Hexagenia limbata, but fly-fishers know it as the Hex. In the midsummer twilight, countless nymphs leave their silty burrows in the stream bottom and emerge from the river as graceful, adult mayflies. The hatch triggers a feeding frenzy among normally reticent browns, which slash at the surface like tame trout in a hatchery raceway.

Soon the river is alive with surface-feeding trout. I manage to dupe a couple of ten-inch tykes, and miss some strikes from seemingly bigger fish. The slurps and gurgles of feeding trout punctuate the evening stillness. Then I hear another, softer sound, like the patter of rain on leaves. But it isn't raining. Looking up, I see thousands of mayflies fluttering above the river in the fading twilight. I stop fishing for a moment to watch their ethereal mating ritual.

Dick Berge calls them angels. A high school art instructor and fly-tier from Madison, Wisconsin, Berge has a northland cabin that becomes the "Hex Camp" for his fly-fishing cronies every summer. Henry Haugley and Larry Meicher hail from Madison. Chuck Gritzner comes up from Iowa. Carl Bradley drove all the way from New York. Tonight, like every night, they are scattered up and down the river.

I'm using Berge's flies, starting the evening with an upright-winged deer hair pattern that imitates the emerging mayfly dun. Later, I switch to a spent-wing, foam-bodied fly representing a dead or dying mayfly spinner that has fallen to the river. Holding the flashlight in my teeth, I listen to a fish rising just downstream of the spring creek. It's been rising in that spot—a choice feeding lane—for awhile now. Maybe I can catch it.

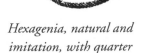

Hexagenia, natural and imitation, with quarter

Sneaking like a deer hunter, I move into a casting position about twenty-five feet upstream from the fish. It's an easy downstream cast. The first try goes short, so I lengthen the line and cast again. There's a slurp and I set the hook. The fish turns with a heaviness that snaps my five-pound tippet. Last night I landed an eighteen-incher, but this fish felt bigger. Why do the big ones always get away?

At 2 A.M. we're back at the Hex Camp and trading stories. It turns out that Larry once broke off a big fish in the very same spot. How big? Like me, he can only speculate. But we both know that monsters lurk in the darkness.

High point of the season

The Hex hatch is the high point of the north-country fly-fishing season, a magic time when most game fish species feed on the surface. The hatch occurs in both lakes and streams. Depending upon latitude and the weather, the peak activity occurs sometime between June 15 and July 15. During a cool summer, you may find the big mayflies still hatching on northern lakes in August.

Hex Dun, White Wing

The sheer abundance of mayflies on some waters is astounding. In communities along the Mississippi River and Lake Erie, snowplows are occasionally required to clear Hexagenia spinners off bridges and roadways. On northern lakes and streams, the spinner fall following a heavy hatch will carpet the water's surface. The Hex is undoubtedly an important food source for trout and other game fish. Abundant mayflies are an indicator of a healthy aquatic ecosystem, because these delicate insects are very susceptible to water pollution. Farm chemicals and other pollutants have greatly reduced mayfly populations in portions of the

Mississippi River. Fortunately, mayflies are still abundant across the North, from the trout streams of northern Wisconsin to the smallmouth bass lakes of Ontario's Quetico Provincial Park.

The Hexagenia spends the first year or two of its life as a nymph burrowed four to six inches into the silt. With sufficient oxygen, the nymphs can live in water depths ranging from one foot in streams to up to fifty feet in lakes. Nymph populations in prime habitat can number in the millions, but the burrowers are out of reach of most fish. In some areas, bait dealers collect Hex nymphs and sell them as Spring Wigglers. The nymphs have feathery gills along their flanks and swim with an undulating action. They are most commonly used for catching panfish and trout through the ice and for spring steelhead fishing on Great Lakes tributaries.

What triggers the nymphs to leave their burrows, swim to the surface, and emerge as mayfly duns? No one is certain. However, experienced fly fishers look for warm, muggy, windless evenings and expect the mayflies to appear just after sunset. Hexagenias occasionally hatch during daylight hours on dark, dreary days. Sometimes, inexplicably, a hatch will occur in one stretch of river, but not in another. A cold front can shut down mayfly activity for several days.

Fishing the hatch in trout streams

Fishing for trout during the Hex hatch is an intense experience. At first you wait and wonder if anything is going to happen. Ten minutes later, every fish in the stream is slashing at the surface. If witnessing a feeding frenzy with a fly rod in hand doesn't charge your adrenaline, take up a new sport.

Hexing neophytes may find the excitement of

A fly by any other name . . .

Hexagenia occasionally goes by other names, such as Shad Fly, Fish Fly, or Michigan Caddis. Whatever they're called, the insects remain essentially the same: mayflies averaging two inches in length, with yellow or cream-colored bodies.

the hatch overrules their fishing sense. With trout seeming to rise everywhere, novices give in to the impulse to make random casts. As a fishing strategy, it's about as effective for catching trout as flock shooting is for hunting ducks. In both cases, the experienced hand picks a specific target. As always, the trout are holding in feeding lanes. They are most likely to take the fly if you make a careful, drag-free drift.

It's a good idea to scout through the stretch you wish to fish during daylight, before the hatch begins. Look for sunken logs, overhanging brush, and other cover that creates choice feeding lies. Then make a few casts to each place to get familiar with the drift. Watch your backcast to see how close your fly comes to the streamside foliage. Once you've practiced your fishing routine in the daylight, doing it in the dark is much easier.

Often you can catch a trout or two before the hatch begins by fishing blind with a Hex dry fly. You can also try subsurface fishing with a Hex nymph or an Olive Wooly Bugger. Typically, though, most fly-fishers prefer to sit on the bank, swat mosquitoes, and wait for the hatch to begin.

The first hatching duns and the first rises ap-

Tips for fishing the hatch
- On streams, scout out a place to fish before sunset.
- If possible, have two fly rods rigged and ready to fish.
- Keep your extra flies in an easily accessible container.
- Change flies when the one on your line becomes waterlogged.
- Use a fine-mesh landing net to minimize injuries to the fish if you practice catch-and-release.
- Don't forget a flashlight and insect repellant!

pear just before sunset. Often these early rising trout seem to cruise about, taking the duns where they find them. As twilight deepens, the activity increases. Duns float the currents like tiny sailboats, with the unlucky ones disappearing in vicious swirls. Watch the rises carefully. Small fish hold in poor feeding locations and attack the mayflies with splashy rises. Big trout occupy the prime feeding locations and eat their duns with a businesslike slurp.

Watch for the rhythm of the rise. Feeding trout usually establish a consistent feeding pattern. They rise to take a drifting fly and then settle back to their holding position. Several seconds or more will pass before they rise again. Time your cast so the fly drifts down the feeding lane when you expect the trout to rise again.

Don't expect the trout to strike at just anything. Even though the trout are slashing at the surface like piranhas after a water buffalo, they're focused on a specific target. Berge recommends that you pay close attention to the silhouette and size of your imitation. After the hatch has occurred

The Baseball

Fishing becomes very difficult during a heavy spinner fall. Your fake fly must compete with hundreds of naturals, drifting in the current, for the attention of a hungry trout. In this situation, veteran Hexer Henry Haugley of Sun Prairie,
Wisconsin, believes it's best to fish with a fly that stands out from the crowd. He'll tie on a pattern called the Baseball, a bristling mass of spun deer hair that looks like a Hexagenia on steroids. The outsize fly is much larger than the natural spinners, which helps attract the attention of the trout. Sometimes, this is all it takes to draw a strike from a finicky fish.

for several nights, trout in heavily fished streams become increasingly choosy. If they don't seem to like your fly, try another pattern.

Presentation is important. If your fly drifts at a different speed than the current and leaves a tiny wake that fly-fishers call drag, a discerning trout will pass it up. An extra-wary trout may stop rising. Make careful casts and always let the fly—even one with drag—drift downstream beyond the rising fish before you lift it off the water to cast again. Sometimes this is easier said then done, because it hard to see your fly in the darkness. If you miss a strike, change flies and "rest" the fish for several minutes so that it forgets about you and starts rising again. Then you can make a second try.

The dun hatch usually lasts about an hour, although sporadic hatching can occur throughout the night. After awhile, you'll notice that the noisy, splashy rises have been replaced by soft sipping sounds. This means the trout are now feeding on the dead and dying Hexagenia spinners that have mated and are now falling into the stream. You can confirm this by shining your flashlight on the stream (be careful, the beam can scare the fish!) to illuminate the spinners drifting spread-eagle in the surface film. Now it is time to change flies. Put on a spinner pattern to match the flies on the water.

About two or three hours after the duns first appear, the trout activity will start tapering off. Soon, all you'll hear are occasional rises. The hatch is over for another night. Most anglers call it quits, but some linger along the stream into the wee hours of the morning and wait for the trout to start rising again. Occasionally these insomniacs are rewarded with good fishing.

When noisy, splashy rises are replaced by soft sipping sounds, change your fly to a spinner pattern.

Tackle and tippets

Your favorite stream fishing outfit and a floating line will work just fine for fishing the Hex hatch. The most important piece of equipment is your leader. The Hex Camp crew prefers tapered leaders from nine to twelve feet with a 3X tippet. The tippet must be strong enough so you can set the hook with the big flies you'll be using. Always carry extra leaders and tippet material. In the dark, when the action is fast and furious, it's often easier to cut off a tangled leader and tie on a new one than to unravel the mess.

Carry your selection of Hex flies in a separate box. It's a good idea to carry a variety of patterns in different sizes. When you judge the size of your fly, go by body size, not hook size. Many anglers prefer to use Hex patterns tied on large, light wire hooks, because big hooks are better suited to fighting big fish.

Fishing the hatch in trout lakes

A friend of mine once caught and released about ninety rainbows and splake while fishing in a lake stocked with trout during an unusual afternoon Hex hatch. As he packed up to go home, a local bait-slinger asked how he'd done. In a rare moment of honesty, my friend said he'd had a banner afternoon. The bait slinger didn't believe him. He hadn't had a bite. So it goes when you fish the right place with the wrong bait.

Dozens of lakes that support trout have a midsummer Hex hatch. As on trout streams, you can catch the biggest trout available on dry flies during the hatch. And trout in some lakes grow much larger than those in streams. Fly-fishers occasionally catch brook trout over three pounds and rainbow trout over five pounds in north-country lakes.

Fishing the hatch in lakes calls for somewhat different methods. Usually, the Hexagenia mayflies hatch in bays and along shorelines where the nymphs find silty habitat. You'll need a boat, canoe or float tube to reach the good places. If you are new to the lake, look for areas with a silt or muck bottom. If the hatch has occurred for several nights, you may find dead mayflies washed up along shore. At dusk, look for rising fish.

Often the fish feed heavily on emerging nymphs prior to the appearance of the duns. I like to start the evening with a fly called the Sparkle Tail Nymph. A weighted nymph with an insect-green body and a tail of bright green Krystal Flash, this fly must look more like a Hex nymph to the trout than it does to me. I often catch rainbows using a twitching retrieve just a few inches beneath the surface. Last summer, while fishing Trout Lake north of Grand Marais, Minnesota, I continued catching numerous rainbows even after the fish began rising to duns on the surface. Finally guilt (snobbery?) made me switch to a dry fly.

When the duns are on the water, trout seem to lose their caution. Often they'll rise right beside your canoe. The fish seem to cruise just

Missed opportunities

Most northern lakes and rivers support populations of giant mayflies, but the appearance of the big bugs usually isn't greeted with enthusiasm by anglers using conventional tackle. Walleyes, smallmouth, and other fish species feed heavily on the mayflies when they're available and spurn the leeches and minnows offered by anglers. On the other hand, fly-fishers can have a ball catching these fish on flies. Few take advantage of this once-a-year opportunity, because they're off fishing their favorite trout waters.

beneath the surface and rise to mayflies in their path. If the trout are abundant, you can cast out thirty feet or so and wait for a strike. A more effective strategy is to watch the rises, gauge the direction a cruiser is traveling, and cast ahead of it.

Effective flies

In the back of this book you'll find a section that's devoted to effective fly patterns recommended by north-country anglers. Included are a number of Hexagenia imitations, many of which were developed by anglers featured in this book. Imitating the giant mayfly presents the fly-tier/fly-fisher with several challenges. The fly must resemble an outsize insect and be tied from materials that will stand up to the crunching jaws of big trout and other game fish.

Foam Body
Parachute Hex

The most important characteristics for a dry Hex are durability and flotation. It's hard to change flies in the dark, so you want a fly that will hold its shape and continue to float after it's caught a fish or two. Second, your fly should resemble the real thing. Because the Hex is so big, many fly patterns call for a body that extends beyond the bend of the hook. Closed-cell foam and deer hair are most often used to construct the bodies. Because foam is softer and more similar in texture to the natural fly, many anglers believe it is more effective than deer hair.

Hexagenia nymphs have an undulating swimming motion that is difficult to mimic with an artificial fly. Although some fly-tiers go to great lengths to create hinged flies that closely imitate the natural, a more practical solution for fishing is to use a Wooly Bugger or large, light-colored nymph. Usually the nymphs are available to the fish for a just short time prior to the appearance of the duns. Actively feeding fish will readily strike

Wooly Buggers and other nymphs fished with a slow, twitching retrieve.

Emergers are very effective at times. In fact, Dick Berge has found that brown trout sometimes inhale emergers so deeply that they cannot be released. An emerger pattern rests in the surface film and represents a dun struggling to shed its nymphal case. You can fish an emerger with tiny twitches to imitate the real thing.

Flex Hex Nymph

Still Water Runs Deep

Trout in lakes

It is a privilege to fish in the company of loons. On still evenings, they serenade fly-fishers with a weird, primal laughter as ancient as the northern lakes. Sometimes loons swim close and then dive near the canoe, gliding beneath you with an elegant grace. Fly-fishing, by comparison, is a clumsy way to fish.

Some anglers say that loons on a lake are a sign of good trout fishing.

Some anglers say that loons on a lake are a sign of good trout fishing. Their logic is sound, although it probably isn't scientific fact. Loons eat fish, so a small lake inhabited by loons probably contains a healthy supply of trout and baitfish. Although loons undoubtedly eat trout, they leave plenty for anglers.

Growing numbers of fly-fishers are joining the loons on quiet northern lakes stocked with stream trout. In the dozens of trout lakes along Minnesota's Gunflint Trail, it is common to see fly-fishers casting from canoes or float tubes. The fish they catch reach larger average sizes than trout in most north-country streams. Stream trout from twelve to sixteen inches are common in lakes, and much larger fish are possible.

The sage of the Gunflint fly-fishers is Reuben Swenson, a quiet, thoughtful man who lives from his pickup truck and fishes nearly every day of the year, summering in northern Minnesota and wintering in Arkansas. Due to a serious heart condition, he is unable to work. Swenson is best known to his friends in the Arrowhead Fly-Fishers Club, of which he is president, as the "Frugal Fly-Fisherman," for his propensity to save money on fishing gear. He won't buy anything he can make, and he'll fix up old tackle before purchasing new stuff.

All about trout lakes

North-country lakes are typically stocked with rainbow trout or brookies. Some lakes are stocked with splake, a fast-growing brook trout/lake trout hybrid that is produced in hatcheries. Occasionally, hard-to-catch brown trout are released in lakes. Usually, stockings must be continued, because the stream trout cannot successfully spawn in a lake environment.

Some notable exceptions exist in Ontario. The province has a number of lakes that support spawning brook trout populations. Most lakes with wild brook trout are closed to winter fishing to give the fish some respite from anglers. The Lake Kirkpatrick or Blue Lake system north of Elliot Lake, Ontario, has a unique population of self-propagating rainbows, as well as wild brookies. The rainbows, which average about four pounds at adulthood, behave like steelhead, the seagoing rainbows of the Pacific Northwest. They spawn in tributary creeks and spend their adult life in the lake.

Most trout lakes are small and deep enough that they remain fairly cool throughout the summer. Usually the lakes contained no game fish before trout were introduced. Occasionally these lakes become overrun with suckers, perch, or baitfish and must be "reclaimed" through the use of a short-term fish poison. Some lakes, called two-story lakes, have warm water species such as bass and panfish living in the shallows, while stocked rainbow trout lurk in the depths.

Swenson does most of his fishing from a float tube, which he can easily carry down the short, rocky paths that lead to many trout lakes. He estimates that he spends three hundred hours a year in his tube. "Once you try a float tube, you become entranced with it," he said. Perhaps that accounts for the tube's popularity among still-water trouters on the Gunflint. Float tubes are made to order for these small lakes, most of which are less than a half mile in diameter. Tubers have a lower profile than anglers in boats or canoes, a stealthy advantage in these clear waters. Often fly-fishers in canoes find there is a "dead zone" around their craft, because the trout see them and spook away. By contrast, Swenson says he sees trout rise within a few feet of his tube.

Although northern trout lakes support mayflies, caddis flies, dragonflies, and midges, most insect hatches are sporadic. Early in the season, trout feed on midges and other small aquatic insects. During June, the trout eat large dragonfly nymphs, which are abundant in many lakes. Large Brown Drake mayflies hatch in the evening during the latter part of the month, followed by Hexagenias. Sporadic Hex activity may continue until early August. During the summer you may find the trout feeding on small tan moths or flying ants. Various-sized floating caddis patterns will catch fish all summer. Try fishing with them near shoreline brush. Some lakes have Blue-Winged Olive hatches in August and September. Expect late season trout to be selective.

The fish have other sources of food such as minnows, leeches, crayfish, and scuds (freshwater shrimp) available throughout the open-water season. Try fishing minnow imitations in spring and fall, and leeches and crayfish during the summer.

Crayfish patterns should be fished among the shoreline rocks.

Soft flies

Whiskey Fly

"We pay attention to what the fish is doing, but we should focus more on what the bait is doing," says St. Paul, Minnesota, angler and fly-caster Bob Nasby.

He believes that many flies look good in the fly box, but appear stiff and lifeless in the water. Nasby's own fly box is stuffed with soft, fuzzy, fluffy flies for still-water fishing. One of his favorites is the Whiskey Fly, a simple, yet deadly, pattern. To tie the Whiskey Fly you need only one material: wild turkey (hence the name) marabou. In your hand, the Whiskey Fly looks like something swept out of a dusty corner, but in the water the delicate marabou flutters and breathes. To a trout, the fly resembles any number of critters that are good to eat.

Soft materials such as marabou, rabbit fur, Hungarian partridge feathers, hen hackle, chenille, and fuzzy dubbings are key ingredients in still-water flies. Trout in streams have less time to inspect a fly as it drifts with the current and can be fooled into striking a lifeless imitation of the

Favorite flies

Most still-water trouters carry a selection of soft, fuzzy flies and traditional trout patterns. Flies like the Wooly Bugger, Whiskey Fly, Carey Special, Muddler Minnow, and Picket Pin are consistently effective for subsurface fishing. You should also carry standard dry flies like the Adams, Elk Hair Caddis, Blue-Winged Olive, Mosquito, Quill Gordon, and Light Cahill. In late June and early July, be sure to bring a selection of Hex duns and spinners. Include some nymphs like the Hare's Ear, Pheasant Tail, Casual Dress, and Zug Bug.

real thing. In lakes, you must make a sunken fly come alive with your retrieve. A fly tied with stiff rooster hackles moves through the water like a block of wood. But a fly tied with soft hackle or marabou swims like a living nymph.

That's why the Wooly Bugger works so well. When you are fishing for stream trout in lakes and are unsure what the fish are eating, it's hard to go wrong with a Wooly Bugger. In fact, the Wooly Bugger is probably the most popular still-water fly pattern. The key to the fly's effectiveness is the long marabou tail, which has a seductive, lifelike action in the water. Although fly-tiers understand that the marabou tail brings the fly to life, they pay less attention to the hackles that are wrapped the length of the hook, often, choosing dry fly hackles that make the fly as stiff as a bristle brush.

Wooly Bugger

If you follow Nasby's advice, soft hackle creates a more lifelike fly. When you tie Wooly Buggers, choose saddle hackles that are too soft to float a dry fly. Tie the tip of the hackle at the base of the tail and then wrap forward so that the longest hackle fibers are near the head. The result is a fly with a streamlined taper and a more natural appearance. Although conventional trout flies are quite small, Wooly Buggers for fishing trout lakes can be anywhere from an inch and a half to over three inches long. Natural trout foods such as leeches, dragonfly nymphs, crayfish, and minnows are hardly minuscule.

Another effective material for subsurface flies is the white-tipped hair from a gray squirrel tail. The soft hair pulses as it is pulled through the water, and the white provides extra attraction. One of Swenson's favorite still-water patterns is a traditional wet fly called the Picket Pin, which has a gray squirrel wing over a soft, palmered hackle.

His friend Karl Kaufman ties a simple Gray Squirrel Streamer that is equally effective.

Getting down

Although he's known as a fly-fishing innovator, Bob Nasby can be slow to change. One of his fishing friends consistently caught trout in lakes using full-sinking fly lines, but Nasby was reluctant to give them a try. Finally, he did. Now he's convinced no still-water angler should be without them. What made him change his mind? Fishing success. Fly-fishing in lakes with a floating fly line is one-dimensional, because you can only fish on or near the surface. Sinking fly lines in various densities add the dimension of depth to your fishing. You can fish from just beneath the surface to depths of twenty-five feet or more.

Nasby recommends that you carry at least two sinking lines. The first is an intermediate line, which sinks about a foot beneath the surface. If you frequently fish with Wooly Buggers, soft flies, or small streamers, the intermediate could well become your workhorse still-water fly line. Wind and waves affect a floating fly line creating a belly in the line. With an intermediate line you keep direct contact with your fly, so you can better detect strikes and set the hook.

Your second line should be capable of sinking to greater depths. Consider this line your ace in the hole when you can't find trout feeding near the surface. Use this deep sinker to probe submerged points, deep weedbeds, and other promising areas. Nasby's found fast action for rainbows by fishing deep with his Whiskey Fly. Try this method at midday, when the trout go deep to avoid the sunlight.

Fishing with sinking lines can be a pain in the neck. You have to know the sink rate of the

Sinking lines add another dimension to fly-fishing.

particular line you're using, and then patiently count down after every cast so the line sinks to the depth you intend to fish. And you have to strip in most of the line in order to pull the fly from the water and make another cast. You can use intermediate lines with 4- or 5-weight fly rods, but heavy, fast-sinking lines are best fished with 6- or 7-weights. Although less versatile than full-sinkers, sink-tip fly lines are somewhat easier to cast. You can fish a fly at a consistent depth with a full sinking line, but you'll pull the fly toward the surface as you retrieve a sink tip.

Brook trout secrets

"The bigger the fly, the bigger the fish you catch," says expert fly-tyer Dave Asproth of Grand Marais, Minnesota.

Asproth knows what he's talking about. Tacked to the wall of his fly-tying area are snapshots of some of the trophy brook trout he's caught in Minnesota lakes—potbellied brutes running from three to over five pounds. His favorite fly is a Black Wooly Bugger with copper tinsel in the tail and in the body.

"It's worked everywhere I've tried it," he said.

Asproth fishes for northern Minnesota brook trout from the spring opener until the season closes in the fall. In May, the brookies are best taken with bait or spinning gear. You can start catching them on flies around Memorial Day, although you won't see much surface activity. Asproth likes to fish along the shoreline using a sinking line and flies that imitate damselfly and dragonfly nymphs. He fishes them along the bottom at depths of twelve to fifteen feet, which is about the point where you can no longer see the bottom in these clear lakes.

The fishing improves as summer progresses. The best dry fly action is during late June and early July when the Hexagenias are hatching. However, he has his best fly-fishing for big brook trout and splake in late July and early August, a time many would consider the trout-fishing dog days. Perhaps most of us are unwilling to put in the time necessary to fool a true trophy. Asproth has sometimes fished for several days in a row without even getting a strike. His persistence was rewarded with a flurry of action that netted him more than one trophy fish. He and other anglers have noted that big brookies seem to occasionally "turn on" for short periods when they aggressively take flies.

Reading the rise

In streams, feeding trout take a position in the current and then rise to strike insects drifting downstream. In still water, trout swim about as they feed. You have to place your fly where you think the trout will rise next. Still-water anglers must learn to "read the rise." Sometimes, such as during a heavy hatch, this is easy, because the cruising trout make a sequence of rises. Sporadic risers are the most difficult to predict. You can learn to discern a trout's line of travel by watching the rise. Often the back and sometimes the tail of the trout break the surface, and you can see which direction the fish is swimming. Cast your fly five or ten feet ahead of the cruising trout and get ready for a strike.

Sometimes, consistent rises appear in a small area, perhaps the size of your living room. If the rises are beyond casting range, study them before attempting to move closer. Do the rises appear to be made by one fish or more than one? What are they taking? Most important, can you sneak within casting distance without spooking them? Plan your fishing strategy before you begin your stalk.

"You have to be there when it happens," says the patient Asproth.

Where are they?

Even seasoned trouters find still-water stream trout perplexing. In a stream, it's usually easy to figure out the places where the trout hide and feed. On a lake, the trout could be anywhere. You may see trout rising within a few inches of shore or out in the middle of the lake. And the feeding fish may be near the top or more than twenty feet beneath the surface.

Common sense will help you find the fish. What are the trout likely to be eating? Unless you see rises, most likely minnows, nymphs, and other aquatic critters appear on the menu. Try fishing in places where the fish can find something to eat—off points, near weedbeds, or along the shore-line. Each species seems to prefer certain locations. Look for rainbows near weeds and in bays. Brookies often frequent areas with boulders on the bottom. Splake like reefs and points. Brown trout feed very close to shore. Many anglers like to fish along windy shorelines, believing the waves wash food to the waiting trout.

The fine art of trolling

The wind was whipping across Moose Lake so hard that we could hardly make forward progress with the canoe. Somewhere beneath us in this Ontario lake swam brookies as fat as paddle blades. But fly-casting in the gale was frustrating. So we trolled.

I tied on my favorite lake fly: a #10 Olive Wooly Bugger. Then I stripped out about sixty feet of floating fly line. My friend, a spin-fisherman, tied on a plug. Our strategy was practical, but hardly scientific. We headed for the lee side of the lake to get out of the wind. As we crossed a

Depthfinders

Use a portable electronic fish-finder to learn more about the lakes where you fish. Although fish swimming beneath you will appear on the readout screen, these units are best used to locate trout-attracting structures such as reefs and drop-offs. Watch your fish-finder as you paddle around the lake, and make a mental map of the underwater topography.

shallow bay, I hooked a fish. At first it seemed small, then it started taking line. A few minutes later, I slid the net beneath a three-pound speck.

Trolling flies for trout works. A popular technique with earlier generations of anglers, trolling has gained new popularity among float-tube users who fish for still-water trout. Fish in lakes are often scattered, and trolling is an effective way to cover lots of water. At times, trolling vastly outproduces other fishing methods. My friend Ken Kettunen and I once spent a couple of hours casting in vain for rainbows. Then I caught one as my fly trailed behind the canoe while I paddled to a new location. We started trolling, and caught twelve-inch rainbows as fast as we could land them, with the same flies we'd been casting.

"Let's go home," said Ken after we'd landed a dozen or so. "This is getting boring."

He was right.

Slumming it

One of the best in the trolling business is Dick Lenski of Duluth, Minnesota. To a purist, his methods may seem crude, but he is a member in good standing of the Arrowhead Fly-Fishers. Perhaps they look the other way when he pulls out the worms. Lenski's trolling "pattern" is a deadly combination of bait, spinner, and fly. And he fishes—sit down for this—with a spinning reel mounted on a venerable Fiberglas fly rod.

Sometimes I wear dark glasses and go fishing with him. He fishes from a small, lightweight canoe powered with an electric trolling motor. His favorite fly is the Wooly Bugger. He strings a tiny willow leaf spinner on a short monofilament leader ahead of the fly; hangs an inch-long chunk of nightcrawler, "for scent," from the hook; and weights the rig with a couple of small split shot

Spinner Fly

pinched to the line about eighteen inches above the fly.

He usually trolls fairly quickly along the shoreline. Often he finds active fish concentrated in one particular area and then makes passes back and forth. Lenski, who releases most of his catch, often outfishes everyone on the lake. Fly-fishers, especially if they're using floating lines, have difficulty reaching the ten- to fifteen-foot depths where he's fishing. And conventional spinning lures can't match the effectiveness of a spinner-fly.

Lenski says you should pay more attention to the trolling technique than to the particular fly pattern. Although fond of black wooly buggers, he uses other flies in various colors. Most days, one color or pattern will outproduce the others. He likes to experiment and improvise until he discovers what the trout prefer. Lenski is nonchalant about his fishing success. "If it's a good day, you'll catch fish," he says.

Reuben's trolling alternative

Unlike his fishing partners, Reuben Swenson never drags a fly behind him as he kicks along in his float tube. When you troll with a floating or sink-tip line, as many anglers do, your fly travels at a constant level not far beneath the surface. According to Swenson, there's a better way to fish.

"I'm always stripping in my fly," he says. "You have more control that way."

Swenson frequently fishes with a sink-tip line. He casts out, and then patiently waits for the line and his fly to sink as deep as twenty feet. Then he begins his retrieve. When his fly is about twelve feet from the surface, he lets it sink again. He continues this process as he moves along in his float tube, keeping the fly in the prime fishing zone. In order to make it easier to detect strikes, he fishes

Trolling tips

- Use your fly rod to twitch the fly as you troll.

- Vary your trolling speed.

- Troll along the edge of weedbeds and drop-offs.

- Taking a zigzag course is usually more productive than trolling in a straight line.

with a short leader, three and a half or four feet in length, made from 2X or 3X tippet material.

Over the portage

As is true with all trout fishing, the harder it is to reach a trout lake, the better the fishing should be. Due to liberal, nearly year-round fishing regulations designed by fish bureaucrats to "optimize fishing opportunities" rather than provide good fishing, the majority of trout lakes receive heavy fishing pressure. Stream trout bite readily throughout the winter, which makes them a popular ice-fishing target. Even seemingly remote lakes may be easily accessible via snowmobile or dogsled. The winter harvest on some lakes undoubtedly exceeds the summer catch.

Because most lakes receive annual stockings, you can catch lots of trout even in heavily fished waters. What you won't catch are trout that have survived a couple of fishing seasons and grown to larger sizes. Since the trout you catch are usually the products of the most recent stocking, they are often nearly identical in size. Now, there's nothing wrong with catching lots of eleven-inch

Choosing fly rods

If you get serious about still-water trouting, start saving your pennies. No one fly rod can handle all the situations you'll encounter while fishing in lakes. For instance, a 4-weight is the ticket for making delicate presentations, but won't cut the mustard when you're fishing deep. A 6-weight is the best choice as an all-around rod, because you can use it with floating or fast-sinking lines. I do most of my still-water fishing with 5-weights, but use a 7-weight for the heavy work. Regardless of the weight, most lake fly-fishers seem to prefer nine-foot rods because they are easy to cast. Some float-tube anglers use ten-foot and longer rods to keep their backcasts off the water.

brookies, but the fishing is more fun if you stand the chance of nailing an occasional eighteen-incher.

You have to work for the big ones. The departments of natural resources in Minnesota, Wisconsin, and Ontario can provide you with lists of lakes that are stocked with trout. The next step is to locate some potential hot spots on a map. Look for lakes you can't reach by road. If they're closed to winter fishing or inaccessible by snowmobile, better yet. A call to the local fisheries office or a tackle store might be helpful at this point, but don't count on it. Trophy trout are so special that even fish managers seem reluctant to talk about them. Take the advice of other anglers with a lot of salt. People who fish for trout are habitual liars. Honest.

Big rainbows—over sixteen inches—are easier to find than big brook trout. Rainbows grow fast, are less tasty than brookies, and are somewhat more difficult to catch in the winter, all characteristics that favor growing big trout. Brook trout fishing is best in Ontario. You can take it from there.

Traveling light

Keep your extra gear to a minimum, because all it does is get in the way. If you fish from a boat or canoe, you can wear a fishing vest or carry your flies and gadgets in a small tackle box. Chest packs are excellent for keeping your gear dry and handy when fishing from a float tube.

Fishing for Rough Fish
Whitefish and herring

Sometimes you're there when it happens. Such was the case on a cold Memorial Day several years ago. For three days we braved wind and rain to troll for lake trout. On Monday afternoon the wind suddenly died and the sun came out. As we trolled across the lee of a rocky island, we saw fish rising where the subsiding chop met the quiet water.

We had a fly rod in the boat, so we reeled up the trolling lines and went over to investigate the rises. The warming sun had triggered an intense midge hatch among the shoreline rocks. The insects were blown into the lake, where they collected on the "current line" where the waves met the lee. Big fish were slurping them down with the culinary abandon of feasting Romans.

Soon my #16 Adams was floating among the naturals. The first strike was immediate, but the tippet snapped from an overeager hook set. Shakily, I tied on another Adams. Another fish struck on the second cast. This time, the tippet held. A couple of fine runs and a few minutes later, I boated a three-pound lake whitefish. Since we had only one fly rod, I passed it to my friend Alan Lutkevich. He hooked and landed a three-pound

One angler's trash is another angler's treasure.

lake trout with one cast. Then he gave the rod to my father, who doesn't fly-fish. Although he couldn't cast more than twenty feet, Dad lost several flies to ferocious strikes. He was still trying to catch a fish twenty minutes later when the sun disappeared, the wind returned, and the hatch ended as quickly as it began. So goes fly-fishing on the deep, cold lakes of the North. You won't often find the fish feeding on the top, but when you do . . .

Unfortunately, species such as lake whitefish and herring (also called cisco or tullibee) are little appreciated by north-country anglers, who consider them rough fish. The whitefish populations in some lakes have been gill-netted into oblivion to make room for more "desirable" fish like walleyes. But one angler's trash species is another angler's treasure, as anyone who's ever caught a four-pound whitefish on a fly rod can attest. And fresh whitefish or herring filets are white, flaky, and tasty. Both fish are delicious when smoked.

Poor man's grayling

We call the lake herring that we catch on dry flies around the Fourth of July poor man's grayling. The herring and the grayling are related, and they share a shimmering ephemeral beauty when you lift them from the water. Like a grayling's, the herring's silvery flanks show tints of lavender, rose, and other soft hues that quickly fade when you kill the fish. Herring are fragile fish. You must cook or smoke herring while it is fresh, because it soon loses its delicate flavor.

I was introduced to herring fishing by my friend Ken Kettunen of Grand Marais, Minnesota, on Greenwood Lake. On long midsummer evenings, the herring, which average twelve to fourteen inches, move into bays and shallow shoreline areas to feed on hatching mayflies and other insects. They also feed on top early in the morning. Often you'll see dozens of rises, both soft dimples and splashy swirls. The evening activity lasts until dark. Ken likes to fish with a foam-body mayfly imitation of his own design. The fly has gray quill wings made from wing feathers he collects from road-killed herring gulls.

Herring are not always easy to catch. They'll shy away from a boat or canoe, so sometimes long casts are required. Herring have small, delicate mouths, and are difficult to hook. You must play them carefully or the hook will tear free. Kettunen has found it is a good idea to pause before setting the hook when you get a strike. He learned this one evening when the herring seemed to be striking short. Frustrated, he stopped fishing and watched the herring rise to real mayflies. The fish first slashed at a floating insect and then turned to take the fly as it sunk.

Same fish, different names

Pop quiz: What's a medium-sized silvery fish that is an important forage species for pike and walleyes, and is fun to catch on a fly rod to boot? Depending on where you go fishing, that fish might be called a cisco, a lake herring, or a tullibee. Although they may vary somewhat in appearance from lake to lake, they're all the same fish. Biologists usually call them ciscoes.

Ciscoes are open-water, or "pelagic," fish that frequently travel in a large school. Distant relatives of trout, they need cold water to survive. In the summer, they inhabit deeper portions of the lake, although they'll swim to the surface in the morning and evening to feed on insect hatches. Ranging from less than six inches to over sixteen inches in length, ciscoes are a nutritious food source for game fish. Walleyes, lake trout, pike, and muskie grow to trophy sizes on a cisco diet.

"They slap it with their tails," Kettunen likes to say.

Sometimes it's too windy to fish with dry flies. Alan Lutkevich and I confronted that situation one dreary, rainy evening. Once, the wind calmed down enough that we were able to raise several herring in short succession. When the wind returned, Lutkevich switched to a cream-colored weighted nymph. He soon discovered the herring were feeding just beneath the surface and managed to land two before the wind and rain chased us off the lake.

You can catch whitefish on flies during the summer, too. Dawn and dusk are the best times to look for them. Whitefish often cruise just beneath the surface, rising to floating mayflies and other insects in their path. When you hook a whitefish, hang on. They can run from two to five pounds or more and are strong fighters.

Spring whitefish

In Ely, Minnesota, fly-rodders make their first casts shortly after ice-out. Within a seven to ten days after the ice disappears, whitefish move to the shallow shoals off river mouths to feed on what local newspaper editor and outdoor writer Bob Cary calls a "small grayish-white grub." Fishing action can be fast and furious.

"On a good day, two fishermen can hook about sixty, land and release twenty, and keep a couple of whitefish to eat," Cary said.

Cary fishes for whitefish with a very simple fly: just a wisp of badger fur or gray squirrel tail tied to a #12 hook. He sometimes ties the fly on a $^1/_{32}$- or $^1/_{64}$-ounce jig so that it sinks better. The fishing technique is simple too. Just drift the fly in the current where whitefish are feeding. When you get a strike, lift your fly rod to set the hook and hold on. Whitefish frequently make a strong, fast run. Don't try to stop them.

The fishing action near stream mouths lasts until early June, when surface water temperatures warm and the whitefish begin moving toward deeper water.

If you want to keep a couple of whitefish for a meal, Cary offers this advice: put your catch in a mesh bag rather than on a stringer. Whitefish struggling on a stringer may attract a large and hungry northern pike. Cary claims a fishing friend was once pulled off balance when a pike grabbed a whitefish attached to a stringer hanging from his belt while he waded and fished near a river mouth. No one wants to be dunked by a pike!

Whitefish

Maverick Sport

Northern pike and muskie

Eric DiCarlo is a maverick. In northern Ontario, everyone has a V-hulled boat. Not Eric. He runs a sixteen-foot flat-bottomed johnboat. Around his home in Wawa, on Lake Superior's northeastern shore, most anglers fish for walleyes and brook trout on inland waters or troll for lake trout and salmon on the big lake. Again DiCarlo departs from the norm. He likes to fly-fish for northern pike. And he finds the johnboat's open deck is an excellent casting platform.

We're drifting in Eric's boat along the deep edge of a submerged weedbed on sprawling White Lake, near the northern Ontario town of White River. DiCarlo is casting a fly-fisherman's version of a jerk bait, a huge foam popper he tied himself. The popper has a wedge-shaped head, so it dives and gurgles as he retrieves it.

In the past, DiCarlo has caught and released as many as four dozen pike here on a single afternoon. He says some of the northerns, which run four to ten pounds, leap completely out of the water when they strike the fly. Today, however, a slight chop on the water limits the popper's effectiveness. DiCarlo doesn't raise a fish.

These tough fighters need tarpon tackle and a bionic casting arm.

Northern Pike

Foam Popper

The tackle we're using is suited to tarpon. My 9-weight fly rod is outfitted with a 10-weight intermediate line designed for tarpon fishing. In fact, the eight-inch yellow-and-red hackle fly I'm casting is actually a tarpon pattern. The fly sinks quickly, and I retrieve it with fast strips along the deep edge of the weeds.

The first strike is a hammer blow. I set the hook and the fish makes a diving run. My fly rod bows deeply. The battle continues for five minutes, ending when I lift a seven-pound northern into the boat. Fly-fishing for pike, I decide, is a whole lot of fun. A few minutes later, I catch a six-pounder. The active fish seem to be located on an inside turn in the weedbed. Two casts later, something removes both my fly and the ten-inch wire leader on the strike. Pike aren't shy when they attack a fly.

Although Ontario waters typically have more and larger pike than U.S. lakes, you don't have to travel to Canada to catch pike—or muskie—with a fly rod. Any place where pike are catchable with conventional tackle and artificial lures, you can probably catch them on flies. Just have realistic expectations about the size and numbers of fish that you'll catch. The only trick to catching pike with a fly rod is tying flies durable enough to stand up to these toothy fish. DiCarlo's foam popper fills the bill.

He starts by carving a wedge-shaped head out of dense closed-cell foam. His favorite source of foam is a pair of beach sandals he bought on sale at Canadian Tire. He glues hobby eyes to the head to make it more realistic. The head is secured to a long-shanked #2/0 bait hook he also found at Canadian Tire. A tail of six brightly colored saddle hackles completes the fly. DiCarlo says you can catch a dozen pike on one popper before it falls apart. It's a maverick pattern from a maverick fisherman—for a maverick freshwater fish.

Fly-fishing for pike is best in late spring, early summer, and fall. Pike spawn in the early spring. After a short recovery period they begin feeding on suckers, shiners, and other spring-spawning baitfish. Pike prefer cool water, and you can find them in the shallows until the hot summer sun drives them into the depths. As the water cools in September, they again become active and accessible to fly-fishers.

Tim Holschlag fishes for pike in rivers during the fall, because they become more aggressive at a time when smallmouth bass are increasingly difficult to catch. Although river pike average less than ten pounds, they're still larger than most of the fish you'll catch with a fly rod. Look for them in

Leaders for pike and muskie

Pike and muskie anglers need a leader that is stout enough to roll over a huge fly and impervious to sharp teeth. You can find commercial tapered leaders designed for pike fishing. Leaders made for bass bugging work, too. Look for leaders with a stiff butt section to turn over the fly. If you build your own leaders, start with a butt section of 50- or 40-pound-test monofilament. Most anglers prefer leaders from five to nine feet in length.

The tippet strength is unimportant because you'll modify it anyway. The simplest method is to cut back the tippet to 15-pound test and then tie on a traditional snap-and-swivel wire leader. The leader won't sink a buoyant popper or affect its action. You can also buy coated cable (at least 20-pound-test), crimps, and a crimping tool to make your own wire tippets. Homemade wire tippets should be a least twelve inches long. A large pike can easily inhale the fly and a short wire leader. Pike and muskie are rarely line shy, so some anglers use a heavy monofilament leader. A 30-pound-test monofilament tippet will hold most pike.

slow waters and near cover. Vary your retrieve until you determine what appeals to the fish.

Pike patterns

Holschlag says pike are easy to catch with flies. He advises that potential pikers use bright-colored streamers "as big as you can throw." Pike are at the top of the aquatic food chain and they like big baits. I once caught a six-pounder that looked like it swallowed a turtle. A filet knife autopsy revealed a ten-inch crappie. Try imitating that with a fly!

Most pike flies are tied on saltwater or similar extra-large hooks. Flies must be big, but not bulky. Saddle hackles are often used to create long, light-weight flies. The hackles should be tied at the rear of the fly and trail out behind so they don't become twisted around the hook bend when you cast. Saltwater patterns like the Sea Ducer and Lefty's Deceiver in white, yellow, chartreuse, or red are good choices. Large bucktails are durable and easy to tie. Simple flies are best, because flies are quickly annihilated by a pike's sharp teeth.

Fly-fishing for muskies

Muskies are called the fish of ten thousand casts. If this is true, the fly-fishers who pursue them must have bionic casting arms. Actually, if you understand muskie habits, they are as easy to catch with flies as they are with conventional tackle. As when fly-fishing for pike, just have realistic expectations about the size and numbers of fish you will catch.

"It's a lot of casting and a lot of work," says fly-fishing guide Roger LaPenter of muskie fishing.

LaPenter says the best time to fly-fish for muskies is in the spring , when aquatic weeds are emerging. The muskies will be in the shallows. Cast your fly toward shore and then strip it back to the boat, varying your retrieve. Often, the fish

Hackle Fly

will follow the fly and strike near the boat. Sometimes LaPenter sticks his rod tip in the water and makes the classic figure-eight sweep used to entice reluctant muskies into striking.

Bob Nasby wants stable summer weather when he goes muskie fishing, so feeding fish will move into consistent locations and be easier to find. He looks for muskies along edges: weed lines, points, and drop-offs. His favorite places to catch muskies are shallow flats that are close to deep water.

"Flats are the dinner table for muskies and other predators," he says.

Bob's rolling retrieve

A very fast retrieve can coax muskies into striking, but you can only strip line so fast. Bob Nasby likes to speed up his fly as it nears the boat to make it appear as if it is trying to escape. When the fly is less than thirty feet from the boat, he throws a loop into his line with a roll cast. Then he quickly strips line. Following the fly line, the fly accelerates as it turns and starts moving away from the boat. When it turns again and starts coming back you can throw another roll cast. A good caster can use this method to work a fly right around the boat.

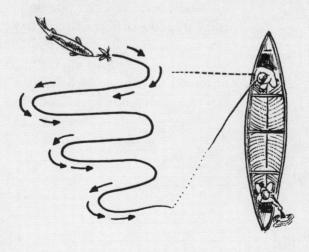

Nasby believes muskies are territorial. Like saltwater barracuda, they'll sometimes follow a fly for twenty or thirty feet, then lose interest and turn away. To cover the water and give reluctant strikers time to take the fly, Nasby frequently makes ninety- to one hundred-foot casts when muskie fishing.

When it comes to flies, Nasby says big isn't always better. Muskies prefer a quick retrieve, and it's difficult to move large flies fast enough. Still, he uses saddle hackle patterns tied on #2/0 to #4/0 hooks. On bright days he prefers white flies with red trim. On cloudy days, yellow and red flies get the nod. In tea-colored, bog-stained water, he favors bright orange. For surface fishing, both he and LaPenter like large Dahlberg Divers.

Tackle tips

Most serious pike and muskie anglers use saltwater fly-fishing gear, because you need strong tackle to cast the monstrous flies. Many fly-rodders use 10-weight fly rods and single action reels with reliable drags. Weight-forward floating or intermediate lines are suitable for most fishing situations, because active pike and muskie can be caught near the surface. Although these big predators are tough fighters, the real workout comes from casting and retrieving the fly. Anglers unaccustomed to fishing with heavy gear may find they're tuckered out after a couple of hours.

When Opportunity Knocks . . .

Walleyes, lake trout, steelhead, and salmon

Fat Hexagenia duns were disappearing in quiet swirls. Were the walleyes rising? Supposedly they were the only game fish species in the lake. There was only one way to find out. Although we were fishing with leeches on spinning gear, I'd brought along a 5-weight outfit and a box of flies. I reeled in the leech and rigged up the fly rod. A few minutes later, my Hex imitation disappeared in a rise. Soon afterwards, I was admiring my first walleye caught on a dry fly. Before darkness fell, I caught three more.

Bottom-dwellers such as walleyes are not typically considered fly rod fish. They rarely feed on the surface and they lack the angler appeal of species like trout or smallmouth bass. Even the most open-minded fly-fishers snub the walleye, perhaps because the fish is so popular with everyone else. Start asking around, though, and you'll find that many experienced fly-fishers have caught walleyes. A few have had exceptional fishing. Most often walleye fly-fishing amounts to being in the right place at the right time: the walleyes were feeding

You can catch more than trout with fly rod and reel.

on the surface or in the shallows and the angler
had a fly rod along. No doubt if more fly-fishers
seriously pursued walleyes, they'd develop techniques to catch them consistently.

One fly-rodder who's caught hundreds of walleyes while fishing for smallmouth bass is Tim
Holschlag. Many of his beloved smallmouth
streams also support native walleyes, and he's
found walleyes will readily strike at a sinking fly.

"If you're fishing on the bottom, you'll catch
walleyes," Holschlag says. "The problem is that
most anglers don't fish deep enough."

Walleye

In the small to medium-sized streams where
Holschlag frequently fishes, walleyes are usually
found in the larger, deeper pools. He catches walleyes in the tailouts (downstream portion) of pools.
Because their eyes are sensitive to sunlight, the
walleyes are most active during low-light periods.
To catch walleyes, Holschlag fishes upstream with
jiglike dumbbell-eyed flies like the Rabbit Strip
Leech and the Wooly Bugger. He uses a floating
line and strike indicator, and retrieves the fly with
the current. If the indicator hesitates or dips beneath the surface, he sets the hook.

Sometimes you can catch walleyes where a
stream flows into a lake. These areas attract spawning walleyes in the spring. Following the spawn, a
few walleyes linger in or near the stream if food is
available. In the fall, walleyes again congregate in
the currents. Stream mouths are particularly attractive to fly-fishers because they are usually fairly
shallow. This makes it easy to present your fly to
the fish. The best fishing will probably be at dusk
and after dark, when the walleyes slip into the
shallows. Be sure to keep your fly near the bottom. Leeches and streamer patterns will fool them.

If you understand the habits of walleyes, you
should be able to catch them on flies in lakes.

Many north-woods lakes have abundant walleye populations. These fish follow a predictable feeding pattern. Although they may feed during the day in bog-stained lakes, more often they spend the daytime hours loafing in deep water. Just before dark, schools of feeding walleyes move toward shore. You can intercept them off points and along the edges of shallow shoals. Use an electronic depthfinder to locate the schools. Nine times out of ten, walleyes will be right on the bottom. That's where your fly should be, too.

Last summer, I heard of a fly-fisherman who caught several sizable walleyes in Quetico Provincial Park using a sinking fly line, a short leader, and a Muddler Minnow. The sinking line snaked along the bottom, while the buoyant Muddler floated up a few inches. The method was similar

All about walleyes

The best walleye lakes are relatively shallow, windswept, and at least one thousand acres in size. The constant wave action keeps the gravel clean in shoreline spawning areas. Although they are native to most northern watersheds, walleyes have been stocked beyond their natural range. For instance, walleyes were introduced to many lakes in the Boundary Waters Canoe Area Wilderness decades ago. Because these lakes have clean gravel, naturally reproducing populations have thrived.

No fish nears the walleye in popularity among north-woods anglers. They are considered one of the best-tasting freshwater fish. Even though walleyes spawn successfully in most northern lakes, anglers often demand that fish managers stock large numbers of hatchery-raised fish. But the stocking may have little effect on fishing success. The Minnesota Department of Natural Resources, which operates the world's largest walleye hatchery system, estimates that massive statewide stockings contribute less than 10 percent of the state's annual walleye harvest. Nature provides the rest.

to the conventional walleye fishing technique, in which anglers use floating jigs to lift their leeches or other baits off the bottom.

Occasionally, you'll hear intriguing stories about walleyes being taken on bass bugs or poppers. This is most likely to occur during the Hex hatch or in late summer, when the walleyes are feeding on frogs. Roger LaPenter says walleyes usually prefer yellow poppers. He knows of one northern Wisconsin lake where you can catch walleyes on yellow poppers in the evening all summer long. What's the name of the lake? Ask Roger.

Lake trout

The trollers were outfishing us. When we met for dinner at Blue Fox Camp, they told us stories about the lake trout they were catching by dragging hardware and bait behind the boat. We had no stories; not even about the ones that got away. The waters were ice-free, but winter's chill still lingered. The rainbows we sought in Ontario's Lake Kirkpatrick had just finished spawning and were unwilling to bite. Although the water temperatures were too cold for rainbows, they were within the comfort range of lake trout. According to the trollers, the lakers were cruising the shallows. Perhaps one could be persuaded to take a fly.

After dinner that evening we boated across the lake to where a sandy point ran out from the shoreline. We drifted off the point while I cast a weighted Wooly Bugger with a floating line. After a cast, I'd let the fly sink several inches and then slowly work it back to the boat. Once I felt a slight tug. Was it a strike? A few casts later I felt a similar pull and set the hook on an eighteen-inch lake trout. Now, an eighteen-incher may not sound like much of a lake trout, but consider this. First, I was fishing with a 5-weight rod. Second, an eighteen-inch brookie or rainbow is a dandy fish. Lakers are trout, too.

Unfortunately, lake trout have developed an undeserved reputation as sluggish fighters. True, they don't make the sizzling runs of a rainbow trout or the gill-rattling leaps of a smallmouth bass, but lakers are battlers nonetheless. Every one that I've caught on a fly rod has been memorable.

Lake trout will readily take streamers, nymphs, and occasionally dry flies. The only drawback is that they are accessible to fly-fishers for only a short time each year. Lakers prefer water temperatures of about 50 degrees, which means that during the summer they retreat to depths so deep that even dedicated dredgers like Bob Nasby don't go after them. The only time you are likely to find them in the shallows is during the spring, when the water is cold.

Streamer

Tradition dictates that lake trout fishing is best immediately after ice-out, when the lakers cruise very shallow water. However, when the ice goes the water is so cold that it even slows the metabolism of lake trout. Although they'll take bait, you may have trouble getting ice-out lakers to strike an artificial fly. However, lake trout remain in relatively shallow water for several weeks. As the water temperatures rise to 50 degrees, the fish become more active and more prone to strike flies.

On bright days, you'll be most likely to catch lakers in the morning and evening. Try fishing near reefs, points, and other structures. Occasionally on calm evenings you'll see lake trout feeding on the surface. More often they feed on minnows, freshwater shrimp, and aquatic insects. Try fishing with streamers, leech patterns, and soft-hackled nymphs from one and a half to four inches in length. Lake trout seem particularly attracted to white, as well as bright colors like chartreuse and yellow. Natural colors like olive, black, and brown work, too.

If the fish you catch are likely to be less than five pounds, you can get by with a 6-weight rod. Go to a 7-weight or heavier rig if there's a possibility of catching bigger fish. A weight-forward floating line is adequate if the fish are near the surface, but a full-sinking line is more versatile. Like walleyes, lake trout are most likely to be near the bottom.

Superior lakers

A handful of fly-fishers consistently catch lake trout in Lake Superior. For the most part, they fish with streamers near river mouths, which attract feeding lakers during May and June. During the summer, lake trout feed near the surface when water temperatures approach 50 degrees. In the fall, they move into shoreline areas to spawn.

Although few fly-fishers pursue them, lake trout have the potential to provide outstanding fishing. They bite readily and are fairly abundant in many lakes. For instance, every spring we fish with spinning tackle in a lake that has a tremendous population of lakers that average seventeen inches. Usually we catch them within fifteen feet of the surface. Next spring, I'm going to haul my float tube in there and see if I can catch them on streamers fished with a sinking line.

Steelhead and salmon

Every spring and fall, steelhead and Pacific salmon make spawning runs in streams that run into Lake Superior and the other Great Lakes. Steelhead—large, silvery rainbow trout—spawn in the spring, although they run some streams during the fall. Chinook and coho salmon, as well as brown trout, spawn in the fall.

Although you can catch steelhead on flies when the water begins warming up in the spring, fly-fishing is best in the fall. Autumn water temperatures are warmer and the fish are more aggressive. Still, special techniques are necessary to present your fly to the fish. Most often the fly—usually a dark nymph or egg pattern—must be drifted along the bottom. Sink-tip lines will get you down, but you may need to clamp split shot to your leader to put the fly where the fish are. Expect frequent hang-ups.

Sometimes, you can catch rainbows or salmon near the river mouth before or after the run. Wade into the lake and fish along the edge of the river current early or late in the day. Sometimes you'll see fish porpoising on the surface. Try fishing with small, nondescript nymphs, dark Wooly Buggers, or bright streamers on a 3X tippet. Sinking fly lines are more effective than floating ones, but be sure your reel has backing beneath the fly line, because a broad-shouldered steelhead or salmon can make long runs.

Wader Wisdom

The art of staying dry

Fly-fishing can be a miserable sport. Just ask anyone who's ever spent a blustery morning standing hip-deep in icy water while wearing a pair of leaky waders. At first you feel a cold wetness. Slowly or quickly—depending on the size of the leak—your boot fills with water. The initial surprise of a wet sensation becomes a sorry soaked feeling most of us haven't experienced since we were potty-trained. If you stand still long enough, numbness settles in, and when you try to walk, your legs feel like clubs.

Leaky waders can ruin a north-woods fishing trip, as can ill-fitting waders or a pair not designed for the conditions you encounter. Fortunately, a number of advancements have been made in wader design and materials in recent years, making it possible for you to find the perfect pair of waders. If you know what you want, you can wind up chest-deep in satisfaction.

How deep? How often? How much?

Before you begin shopping for waders, ask yourself some basic questions. First, how do you plan to use your waders? Will you be fishing small creeks

Waders can put you hip-deep in water or chest-deep in satisfaction.

Boot foot waders

or large rivers? Riding a float tube? Busting brush? Do you plan to wear waders on occasional weekends or every day? How much are you willing to spend in order to stay dry?

The answers to these questions will steer you in your wader search. For instance, if you plan to spend most of your time fishing shallow creeks, a pair of hip waders may be all you need. But if you like to fish for early spring trout and you want to take a float tube after dog days bass, you may need one pair of insulated waders and a lightweight pair intended for summer use. As for prices, you can spend anywhere from fifty bucks to over two hundred dollars on a good pair of chest waders, and somewhat less for hippers. As is true for most fly-fishing gear, buy the best you can afford.

The choices

The world of waders presents diverse choice. You can get hip-, waist- or chest-high models. Some have boots, while others are stocking-footed and require the additional purchase of wading shoes. Boots and shoes may have tread-pattern soles, nonslip felt soles, or even metal-studded soles for sure-footed wading. Wader materials include neoprene, nylon, and other synthetic fabrics, rubber, and canvas. Some waders are insulated and others are designed for hot weather use.

Let's start with the three basic types. Hip waders are easy to slip on and comfortable to wear. Small-stream anglers and other fly-fishers who are active and primarily wade in knee-deep waters often choose hippers. Because they are inexpensive compared to chest waders, hippers make an excellent "entry level" choice. Waist-high waders are relatively uncommon. You can wade a little deeper than with hippers, without the extra bulk of chest waders. Waist-high waders are a good choice for hot weather, because they are more comfortable to wear than chest-high models.

Chest waders, however, are more versatile. Most anyone who is serious about fly-fishing owns at least one pair. If you plan to stand in water up to your armpits or fish from a float tube, so should you. Chest waders are held up with over-the-shoulder suspenders, although most have belt loops, too. A belt adds a measure of comfort and safety. If you should happen to fall in, the belt helps trap air in your waders so they don't quickly fill with water. Having field-tested this principle on a number of occasions, I can attest that wearing a belt helps you stay dry.

Gotta have some sole

Nowadays, when you see photos of anglers in waders, they are most often wearing stocking-foot models with wading shoes. This combination is comfortable and sturdy, but it may not be for you. Again, give some thought to how you plan to use your waders. Stocking-foot waders, particularly with felt-soled wading shoes, get the nod if you plan to fish hard-bottomed streams and lakes. You should wear gravel-guard cuffs over the top of your wading shoes to prevent gravel from getting between the shoe and wader. Stocking-foots are best suited to float tube use, because they comfortably accommodate swim fins.

Boot-foots are best for icy cold weather and muddy conditions. They are easy to put on and take off, an advantage if you wear them frequently. They are somewhat more clumsy to walk in, but I log many miles in my boot-foots every year with few complaints. Often you have a choice between insulated and uninsulated boots. Regardless of which type you choose, be sure the boot has enough room to accommodate one or two extra

Stocking foot waders

pairs of socks if you'll be wearing them in cold conditions. Cold feet are no fun.

Be sure the soles of your wading shoes or wader boots are suited to the conditions. With boot-foots, a tread sole is most common. This is the best choice for muck, and is suitable for general use. However, if you spend much time wading on slippery rocks or in fast currents, felt soles—available on many boot-foots and most wading shoes—will give you better traction. Felt soles grip the rocks in situations where walking with tread soles is like trying to stand on greased bowling balls. You can make your own felt soles by gluing pieces of indoor/outdoor carpet to your waders with contact cement or by using a commercial felt-sole kit. Experienced stream anglers know that sure footing is often the difference between wading and swimming. In extremely strong currents, even felt soles may not be enough. Metal studs, cleats, or chains are the safest choices for these situations. However, in quiet waters they may make fish-spooking noise as you wade. Cleats and studs wear out with repeated use. For this reason, many anglers choose to buy metal-studded sandals that they can put on and take off as they need them.

What material?

The greatest development in waders in recent years has been the introduction of neoprene. This material, warm, well-fitting, and durable, is made in varying thickness. The greatest drawback to neoprene is that it is prone to tears and punctures. Generally speaking, thicker neoprene is more durable and warmer. Recently, manufacturers have begun marrying neoprene with other materials, such as nylon, for greater strength.

Neoprene waders fit so well that many anglers wear nothing but a pair of long johns beneath

Homemade sandals

My friend Alan Lutkevich made his own pair of wading sandals by gluing a felt sole to a pair of slip-on rubber galoshes and then adding pop rivets for traction. He can carry these handy sandals in the game pouch of his fishing vest and put them on when he needs sure-footed traction.

them. In addition to comfort, a close fit also makes wading in strong currents easier. Those used to wearing several layers of clothing beneath their waders may wonder if they'll stay warm when standing in cold water. Not to worry. In fact, you may find neoprenes are too warm, particularly if you plan to do some walking. Neoprene has a few other shortcomings. Because it tears and punctures easily, sharp balsam and spruce branches slice through it like butter. The material also absorbs water and is slow to dry. If the temperature dips below freezing during the night, you'll be struggling to get into frozen waders in the morning.

Another common wader material is nylon. Nylon is tough, which makes it a good choice for stream anglers or others who may bust brush while wearing their waders. One drawback to nylon is that it doesn't stretch like neoprene, which means sitting or walking is less comfortable. Nylon is sometimes combined with rubber or synthetic materials to add stretch. The lightweight stocking-foot waders preferred by backpackers and travelers are often made of nylon.

Natural rubber has been used to make waders for years. With proper care, rubber waders are long lasting and perform well. One advantage to rubber is that it is easy to clean, something to consider if you'll be wading in places with muck or clay. Although heavier than either neoprene or nylon, rubber waders are often chosen by fishery workers and others who work in waders.

Durability

I once figured that I spent about fifty days fishing and hunting in waders each year, wading streams, standing in swamps, and busting brush. With this hard use, I expect a pair of waders to last at least two years before beginning to leak from deterioration. You can patch waders and continue using them, but eventually they just plain wear out. Since I prefer to spend my money going fishing rather than buying gear, I'm always searching for the ultimate wader—in my case a comfortable boot-foot that can stand up to years of hard use. I've yet to find it, but I keep getting closer each time I purchase a new pair. Manufacturers keep making better waders and I keep becoming a better judge of durability.

The trick to buying durable waders is learning to anticipate where leaks are likely to occur. Leaks can start from punctures, weak seams, or deteriorating materials. Often they begin in stress areas such as the ankle, knee, or (brr!) crotch. When looking at a new pair of waders, pay close attention to the construction of these areas. Carefully check the seams to make sure they are well glued and flexible. The fewer seams, the better.

Punctures are often the wearer's fault. No wader will survive a close encounter with a barbed wire fence or a balsam thicket. But your waders should be able to stand up to the rigors of the north woods. Of course, we all define those rigors in our own terms. A pair of waders that a brush-buster like me would tear to ribbons in a week may be just the ticket for tiding a float tube on roadside lakes.

Deterioration of materials, especially if it occurs within two years of purchase, is usually due to improper storage. One winter I unthinkingly stored a pair of boot-foots near the furnace and the chest freezer. Ozone produced by the electric motors caused the boots to deteriorate and develop fine cracks. In the spring, I had to buy a new pair. Store your waders in a cool, dry place

No wader will survive a close encounter with a barbed wire fence.

away from electrical appliances. You can hang them upside down on a storage rack or fold them for storage in the original box. Take good care of your waders, and they'll take care of you.

Staying Afloat
Float tubes, canoes, and boats

Reuben Swenson has good advice for anyone planning to use a float tube in the north woods: Beware of bull moose and beavers. Apparently, Reuben once attracted the attention of a friendly bull. It was an experience he doesn't care to repeat. On other occasions he's found himself in the company of beavers—and the flat-tails didn't seem friendly. He says you feel somewhat vulnerable when your legs are suspended beneath a float tube while swimming and diving beavers circle around you.

But ornery beavers haven't deterred Reuben nor dozens of other north-country fly-fishers from float tube fishing. In the last decade, float-tubing has become tremendously popular, especially with anglers who fish small, secluded waters. Easily portable, float tubes allow you to fish any lake or pond within walking distance. Best of all, float tubes are the most affordable watercraft on the market. You can get functional entry-level models for less than one hundred dollars or spend over three hundred dollars on a deluxe tube.

Float tubes are not new. Anglers have been making homemade contraptions for decades. The

In a float tube, you feel a bit vulnerable, especially if you find yourself in the company of a moose.

basic concept has remained essentially the same: An angler wearing chest waders climbs into a cradle secured inside an inflated truck tire tube and kicks with swim fins for propulsion. Today float tubes come in two styles: round inner-tube donuts and U-shaped open-front models.

Most anglers are familiar with the donut style. The "bladder," or tube, is covered with a skin made of nylon or a similar material. The outer shell may contain storage pockets, an apron to cover the "donut hole," and even a beverage holder. Many models feature a backrest that is inflated with a motorcycle tire tube. The newer U-shaped float tubes are also covered with a shell. Some have lightweight frames to help hold their shape. The advantage to these open-front models is that it's easier to climb in and out.

Going backwards

The expression "like a duck out of water" certainly applies to float-tubers. With donut tubes, you must put your swim fins on and then climb into the tube. Once you're in the tube, you walk backwards into the water. This is difficult in places with steep shoreline banks or soft lake bottoms. With U-shaped tubes, you can sit down in the tube in shallow water and then put on your fins.

Once you're afloat, tubing is an enjoyable way to fish. First-timers may feel uneasy until they become comfortable with tubing, but usually, the uneasiness passes within a few minutes. Then you can settle down for some serious fishing. Float tubes are surprisingly effective fishing tools, because they allow you to approach the fish. For some reason, fish aren't frightened by float tubes. Wary game fish will let you approach within easy casting distance. This is why float tubes have become so popular with fly-fishers and other anglers who

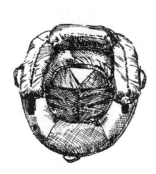

Float tube

like to fish ponds and small lakes. In many situations where a boat or canoe would spook the fish, a float-tuber can sneak right in on the action. In a float tube, you're just part of the environment.

Another advantage to float tubes is their portability. The average donut tube weighs about twelve pounds, and some U-shaped models weigh less than seven pounds. You can leave the tube inflated for short carries or deflate it for easier backpacking. Most tubes can be inflated with a hand or foot pump. You can blow up some like a balloon, although it is difficult to get sufficient air pressure for maximum flotation.

Where can you use a float tube? Although intrepid anglers use them on the Great Lakes and slow-moving rivers, float tubes are designed for lake and pond fishing. The best places for float tubes are small waters with minimal motorboat traffic. This makes them ideal for trout lakes and beaver ponds. On big lakes, you can travel to the place you plan to fish with a motor boat or canoe, tie it up on shore and then go fishing with your float tube. Some tubes have a fluorescent backrest to make you more visible to boaters.

Because the tubes are self-propelled, you are limited by your own physical abilities in the distance you can travel from the access point. An incoming breeze could slow your travel. However, many people who have physical disabilities that prevent them from partaking in strenuous activities like wading or paddling find they can fish very comfortably from a tube. Heavyset individuals can even find specially designed models.

You travel backward in a tube, because you're in a sitting position and kicking with your feet. Some fin styles, usually called kickers, allow you to travel forward, although at slower rates than swim fins. And not all swim fins are created equal.

Generally, the longer fins provide better propulsion. With all styles, it is easy to turn and position the tube for fishing. Some anglers carry a small anchor to hold them in place when fishing on breezy days.

What sort of waders work best with float tubes? Look for models with a front and back bib to minimize splashing. Most anglers prefer neoprene waders, because they are comfortable to wear and will keep you warm when you spend several hours immersed in cold water. You can buy swim fins that fit stocking-foot or boot-foot waders, but stocking-foots are lighter and easier to wear. If you plan to wade and fish, too, you can stow your wader boots on the tube. Frequent tubers, especially those with donut styles, may eventually develop wear marks at the point where the waders come in contact with the cradle.

Fishing from a tube

Fishing from a float tube requires some variation from your standard technique. For instance, you should kick away from the fish when you get a strike to get a solid hook set. Even medium-sized fish can move the tube as you battle them, and an exceptionally large fish may tow you around. Be sure you have a landing net to contain the fish.

Some fly-fishers have trouble casting from a float tube because they are so low to the water. Most experienced tubers prefer fly rods that are nine or even ten feet in length to keep a high backcast. Be extra careful with those sharp hooks when you're casting or landing a fish. No one wants to spring a leak.

Last summer, I was fishing a large lake from my float tube when I heard a soft hissing. A quick check showed the tube was leaking. I started kicking toward the shoreline, which was about a quarter mile away. It was a long ride, but I made it. Although it was tense, I was actually in little danger. My donut tube had a second, smaller bladder in the backrest and I was wearing a life preserver. If the truck tube had deflated, there were people on shore within the sound of my voice.

Place safety first whenever you use a float tube. Always wear a personal flotation device (PFD) and use a tube with two bladders. Whenever possible, tube with a friend. In addition to accidental deflations, a boat wake or large wave can tip over your tube. The U-shaped tubes provide an extra margin of safety, because you can easily get out of the tube. Escape from a donut tube in an emergency situation might foil even Houdini.

Some bladders are better constructed than others. The most leakproof bladders are truck tire tubes made of rubber and specially designed tubes made of urethane. Most experienced tubers don't recommend bladders made of PVC or vinyl. Although these bladders are inexpensive, some are prone to leakage at the seams, and the material becomes brittle in cold weather. Check the valve style when you purchase the tube. Some bladders can be filled with an air compressor and some cannot. You can fill the bladder to optimum air pressure with a compressor.

Take care of your tube and a quality bladder will last several years. Sunlight is your biggest enemy. Keep the tube in a cool, shaded place when not in use. My leak last summer was my own fault, because I left the tube inflated when in storage. When you take the tube out for the season, check the bladder for cracks or signs of wear. Don't take chances with a faulty tube. Why risk your life just to catch fish?

And remember: Beware of bull moose and beavers.

Float tube safety

- Always wear a PFD.
- Tube with a buddy.
- Stay away from waves and strong currents.
- Avoid areas with heavy boat traffic.

Canoes

Canoes are as much a part of the north woods as loons or the northern lights. For centuries, on narrow creeks and vast lakes, they have carried people going fishing. The most versatile craft in a north-country fly-fisher's flotilla, a canoe slips through shallow water, yet it is amazingly seawor- thy. Lightweight and easy to carry, a canoe can be launched virtually anywhere.

The perfect canoe for fly-fishing is a matter of personal preference. Some anglers prefer the clas- sic curves of traditional wood-canvas canoes. Others like the modern ultralight hulls made of space-age materials. Utilitarians may opt for a durable aluminum model. The canoe that's best for you depends on your needs as an angler and, to a certain degree, the depth of your pocketbook.

If you plan to use your canoe to reach wilder- ness lakes, you'll want a craft that is light enough to portage and designed for lake travel. Your needs may be best met with a space-age canoe designed for wilderness travel. If you mostly fish on lakes that you can drive to, your greatest concern may be stability. Foam stabilizers make a canoe virtu- ally impossible to tip. River rats after smallmouth bass need a canoe that can take a battering and will slide over rocky riffles. Aluminum sticks to rocks like a magnet, so a tough synthetic hull is a better choice.

Outfit your canoe for fishing comfort. A good yoke, for instance, will take the pain out of por- taging. A rowing rig or bent shaft paddles increase your efficiency, greatly reducing travel time. On lakes where motors are allowed, consider an elec- tric trolling motor. They're quiet and allow you to continue fishing as you position the canoe. Of course, electric motors are well suited to trolling. Their only drawback is the heavy battery used for power. Deep-cycle batteries simply weigh too much to be carried any distance. Wilderness anglers can pack a sculling paddle, a one-handed blade for propelling and positioning the canoe.

Use an anchor to hold your position on a breezy lake or in river currents. You can purchase a small anchor or make your own. Wilderness anglers usually bring a length of rope and a strong mesh sack. When they go fishing, they fill the sack with rocks for weight.

Fishing teamwork

On streams and lakes, the most effective way to fly-fish from a canoe is if the person in the bow casts while the person in the stern paddles. The paddler controls the canoe while the caster fishes all the likely places. You can occasionally trade positions so both individuals get a chance to fish. Sometimes the stern paddler will find opportunities to make a few casts. On lakes, you can trail a fly off the stern.

The trick to successful teamwork fishing is making sure both anglers understand the rules of the game. Fly-fishing from a canoe is not a sport for the sort of angler who can't enjoy watching someone else catch fish. Choose compatible fishing partners—ones who use methods similar to your own and fish at the same pace. Since catching fish is a team effort, the paddler can get just as much satisfaction from putting the canoe in the right place as the caster does from landing the fish.

Fishing alone from a canoe is another matter. You can either paddle or cast, but you can't do both at the same time. Trying to control the canoe and fish on a breezy day is frustrating. Your best bet is to anchor and fish. An electric motor is also handy for solo fly-fishing, because it frees up your hands. On small waters, the solo angler is better off fishing from a float tube.

Boats

Boats offer fly-fishers a few advantages over canoes. First, you can get where you're going much faster driving a boat powered with an outboard motor than paddling a canoe. Second, boats offer improved stability, which means you can fish standing up. Third, it is easier for two people to fly-fish from a boat.

Although there are more boats per capita in the north woods than just about anywhere else, Eric DiCarlo is one of the few anglers who has purchased a boat specifically for fly-fishing. When Eric bought his sixteen-foot johnboat, he was guiding fly-fishers on Ontario's Michipicoten River. In order to run over shallow shoals, he powered the boat with a 35-horse outboard equipped with a jet propulsion unit instead of a propeller. Now that he mostly fishes lakes for pike and bass, he uses the prop.

The disadvantage to a johnboat in the north woods is that it is meant for rivers and shallow marshes, not wave-tossed lakes. But a johnboat

Remember PFDs!

Be sure to wear a Coast-Guard-approved personal floatation device when fly-fishing from a boat, canoe, or float tube.

Small craft

If you plan to do most of your fishing on quiet ponds, a one-person punt will suffice. Today you can find anything from leaky wooden boats to sleek inflatable craft. Inflatables range from traditional oval models to high-tech pontoons. Most are powered with oars, although you can mount an electric trolling motor or small outboard on some. These solo crafts are best suited to ponds and tiny lakes where it is inconvenient to use a float tube or canoe.

with a carpeted floor makes such an excellent fly-casting platform that Eric can put up with the loss of seaworthiness. You can't fly-fish in three-foot swells, anyway.

Nevertheless, most anglers prefer a V-bottomed boat for fishing northern lakes. A number of excellent craft are manufactured here. The sleek high-powered pike boats so popular with walleye anglers are fine for fly-fishing. The only drawback is that you'll probably have the leech wrangler who owns it for company. A standard aluminum boat with bench seats and plywood decking will suit the needs of most fly-fishers. If you like to stand up, fourteen- and sixteen-footers are considerably more stable than twelve-footers.

Keep the fishing area clear of anything that will tangle your line. When you fly-fish from a boat, you'll strip your line into a pile at your feet. Keep clutter to a minimum, so all you have to worry about is stepping on your line. Stow your extra tackle in an out of the way location. If you fish from the stern, keep your line away from the outboard and the fuel tank, because gasoline will destroy a fly line.

Feather Wisdom

Getting started in fly tying

One winter, a few of us had an informal fly-tying club that met every Thursday evening. We were a "salt of the earth" group that included sawmill workers, a logger, a waitress, a newspaper editor, and a retired railroader. No one spoke Latin or traveled to New Zealand to go fishing. But we all had fun tying flies and later using them to catch fish.

If you fish with flies, sooner or later you'll try making your own. Don't make the mistaken assumption that you need the artistic talent of Van Gogh to wrap feathers on a hook. Nothing could be further from the truth. With practice, even a chimpanzee could tie decent flies—stumblebums like me are living proof.

I started tying flies at about age twelve, primarily because I couldn't afford to buy them. A friend who was the same age was my first instructor, and he'd taught himself by unraveling store-bought flies to see how they were constructed. Now, twenty-some years later, Alan Lutkevich and I still tie flies and go fly-fishing. A boyhood pastime matured into a lifelong pursuit.

You needn't be an artist to tie fish-catching flies.

However, changes have occurred during those two decades. Learning how to tie flies has never been easier. Some north-country sport shops now carry a selection of fly-tying materials. There are even a few honest-to-goodness fly shops, and fly-fishing magazines are sold in bookstores. Sometimes, you can find expert tiers like Dave Asproth or Perry Rowlison teaching fly tying as a night-school course at a local high school. If you cannot find a class, books and videos provide an excellent substitute.

It pays to get some instruction to learn about the tools and techniques before investing in fly-tying equipment and materials. Don't be afraid to fork over some cash, say two hundred dollars, when making your initial investment in fly tying. Buy quality tools once and you're set for life. Shop around because prices vary. Get several mail order catalogs and visit the nearest fly shop. You may pay a little more at the shop, but the personalized service and advice is worth the extra price. Shop smart, avoiding the urge to buy materials that look cool, but that you'll rarely use. Focus on hooks, hackle feathers, dubbing, peacock herl, chenille, floss, tinsel, fine wire, marabou, bucktail, deer hair, and other materials used to tie a wide variety of flies. Again, taking a class or reading some books beforehand will give you a better idea of what to buy.

Hackle pliers

Bodkin

Bobbin

Learning the language

One of my ninth grade teachers was a fly-tier who liked to talk fishing. Perry Rowlison solved a fly-tying mystery that had baffled Al and me in our early efforts—how to make a "dubbed" body. It seems so simple now. You spin some fuzzy fur or similar material around your thread to make a yarn and then wrap it around the hook. The process is called dubbing, and we were stumped by the term.

"Hackle" is another term that baffles beginners. The hackle is the portion of the fly that represents the legs. It is most often made by wrapping a hackle feather around a hook so that the individual barbs separate and stand out like legs. Hackle feathers often come from the necks of chickens, particularly roosters. Feathers with stiff barbs are used to tie dry flies, because they'll float the fly on the water's surface. Soft barbs are preferred for subsurface wet fly and nymph patterns. Hackle pliers are used to wind the feathers around the hook.

Other fly-tying terms are self-explanatory. Anyone who's ever been bitten by a mosquito should be able to identify the tail, body, wings, and head on an artificial fly. And it doesn't take a rocket scientist to figure out that you need a fly-tying vise to hold the hook while you tie a fly. However, beginning tiers will come across confusing terms and techniques as they learn to tie new patterns. For instance, you don't make a badger hackle with badger fur. "Badger" instead refers to a two-toned hackle feather that is dark near the stem and edged with a lighter hue. An illustrated fly-tying reference book—a number of excellent ones are available—will prove an invaluable addition to your angling library.

Sitting down at the vise

When I was a kid, I enjoyed looking at pictures of Atlantic salmon flies. Beautiful, exquisite patterns tied with exotic materials, these flies stirred the imagination of a

Tools You'll Need

- Fly-tying vise
- Hackle pliers
- Sharp fine-point scissors
- Fly-tying bobbin
- Bodkin

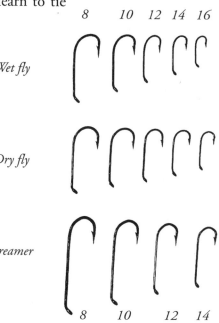

Wet fly

Dry fly

Streamer

young fisherman. But even though a salmon fly such as the Jock Scott is a work of art, it won't catch much on the northern waters where I fish. Practice tying flies that will work where you go fishing. If you already fly-fish, you probably have some favorite flies. Use the flies in your box as patterns for those you tie.

Never be afraid to experiment. Quite often a "souped up" pattern of your own design will out-perform the standard recipe on the waters where you fish. Researching this book, I had the oppor-tunity to peek into the fly boxes of hard-core fly-fishers. I noticed that many tie scruffy, nonde-script flies that only faintly resemble the models in recipe books. These tiers have reduced the fly to its essential elements—the ones that catch fish.

This doesn't mean these tiers are sloppy or lazy. Just because a fly appears scruffy doesn't mean it is poorly tied. A well-tied fly is one that is well proportioned. The tail is neither too long nor too short, the hackle is the right diameter for the hook, and the wings are set at the proper angle. Another quality I always look for in a fly is durability. In fly-fishing you often have fast action for short periods of time. You don't want to spend that time changing flies that have been mangled by fish. Always give finished flies a tough quality check. Be your own worst critic. The result will be ever-better flies.

And, of course, there's no substitute for prac-tice. However, this is rarely a problem for beginning tiers. Most, in fact, become inspired with an almost fanatical zeal as their skills im-prove. Don't be surprised to find yourself sitting at the tying bench until the wee hours of the morning—time flies (pardon the pun) when you're having fun.

Vise holding fly

Material gains

From modest beginnings, my collection of fly-tying materials has grown into a substantial pile of
feathers and fur. However, once I'd made my initial investment in tools and materials, subsequent
purchases were inexpensive and on an "as needed"
basis. I try to keep a mental list of materials I need,
but rarely remember them when I get to the fly
shop. If you discover you need a certain item, write
it down. Use your needs list as a guide when you
place a catalog order or visit a fly shop.

Some fly-tiers make a hobby out of accumu-
lating material. A beginning tier can do no better
than to get to know the local fly-tying curmudg-
eon. Not only will you have an opportunity to learn
from an expert, but that expert may also help you
build up your supply of materials. The collections
of some tiers are truly awe inspiring, and most are
willing to share with a beginner. Just be sure to show
your appreciation for their generosity.

Always keep a sharp eye open for a good deal.
I once found big bags of marabou feathers on
clearance at a lawn and garden shop. I've also
bought useful materials that were being sold as
Christmas decorations, scrubbing material, or
craft items. Occasionally you'll trip across inter-
esting packing materials. Awhile back a friend

Tying tough

Tying more durable flies is simply a matter of paying attention to details. Always make sure that materials are secured
with tight wraps or a half-hitch before you move on to the
next step. Add a drop of cement for extra strength. Use durable materials.
Split quill wings, for instance, are more fragile than wings made of hackle
tips or deer hair.

gave me some cellophane that makes dynamite translucent minnow bodies.

Another source of fly-tying materials at good prices is estate sales. Don't feel guilty about acquiring some fellow angler's lifetime collection of materials on the cheap. The ghost of that fisherman is probably happy someone will put those materials to good use.

Some tiers go so far as to collect their own materials. More than a few have been known to scavenge road kills. I don't think I've ever purchased squirrel tails, duck wings, or pheasant feathers. A few years ago a friend gave me dry fly-quality necks from his own chickens. I doubt if I'll ever start raising chickens, but I have been known to snip a few hairs off the family dog. In fact, I have a sack of husky fur (bless old Smoky's departed soul), which makes dubbed bodies that really float because the fur is so rich in oils. Dave Asproth creates exquisite Hexagenia emergers with bodies made from Styrofoam egg cartons.

In fly-tying, your only limit is your imagination. That's why it is such an absorbing pastime. You can concoct new patterns to represent a particular bug or minnow found in the waters where you fish. Anglers have done so for centuries, and some of those flies became tried-and-true universal patterns. But even if you don't invent the next Royal Coachman, tying your own flies allows you to have the special thrill of catching a fish on a lure you made yourself.

The Best Patterns

A north-country fly box

The following fly patterns were recommended by north-woods fly-fishers as flies that catch fish. Some are original recipes, others are standard patterns or modified versions. Regardless of the origin, the patterns listed are as tied by the angler who suggested the fly be included in the book.

Some patterns suggest using lead wire for weight. However, the federal Environmental Protection Agency is in the process of restricting the use of lead for fishing. In most instances, you can substitute copper wire for lead.

DRY FLIES

Adams
as tied by Karl Kaufman

The Adams is one of Karl's "deadly dozen" flies for north-country trout. It's a favorite of dry fly anglers everywhere.

Hook   Light wire, #12–#18.

Tail   Mixed brown and grizzly hackle fibers.

Body   Gray dubbing.

Wing   Grizzly hackle tips.

Hackle   One brown hackle and one grizzly hackle.

Adams (Hair Wing)
as tied by Chuck Gritzner

Delicate yet durable, the Hair Wing Adams is easy to tie.

Hook   Light wire, #10–#16.

Tail   Bucktail.

Body   Bucktail.

Wing   Bucktail.

Hackle   One grizzly and one brown hackle, mixed.

Notes   The butt ends of the bucktail fibers in the tail are used to make the body. Wrap with thread to secure.

Adams (Yellow-Bodied)
as tied by Shawn Perich

This variation was shown to me years ago by Perry Rowlison of Duluth, Minnesota. The fly has worked well for trout wherever I've tried it.

Hook   Light wire, #10–#20.

Tail   Mixed brown and grizzly hackle fibers.

Body   Yellow dubbing.

Wing   Grizzly hackle tips.

Hackle   One or two Cree hackles.

Backwing Hex
as tied by Dick Berge

This beautiful, durable fly has a white calftail wing that stays visible when dusk steals across the stream.

Hook   Long-shanked #6.

Tail   Three moose mane fibers equal in length to the fly.

Body   Yellowish-olive dubbing, palmered with olive grizzly hackle as wide as the hook gap.

Wing   White calf tail, angling back over the body.

Hackle   Olive grizzly hackle, twice as wide as the hook gap.

Baseball

as tied by Dick Berge

It looks like something from a fly-fisher's fever dream, but Berge says the oversized Baseball draws strikes when natural Hexagenias blanket the water's surface.

Hook   Light wire, #4.

Tail   A half-dozen, long, moose mane fibers and the tips of deer hair used to make the extended body.

Body   Light deer hair, tied as an extended body.

Hackle   A wide collar of flared, light deer hair.

Notes   The deer hair collar should extend from the eye of the hook to the midpoint of the shank. Tie in several clumps of deer hair at the butt ends to form a long, dense hackle encircling the hook. Trim the butt ends as you build the collar.

Black (Negative) Hex

as tied by Henry Haugley

Try this pattern when the fish seem selective or the hatch is so intense that your imitation is floating among a crowd of real mayflies.

Hook   Light wire, #8.

Tail   Black bucktail, equal in length to the extended body.

Body   Black deer hair, tied as an extended body.

Wing   Black deer hair, forming a bullet-shaped head and a divided wing.

Notes   To make the wing and head, clean the underfur from a clump of black deer hair and use a hair-stacking tool to even the length of the tips. Tie the clump just behind the hook eye with the tips facing forward. Wrap your tying thread to a point about one-quarter-inch from the hook eye. Then pull the hair back and secure it with several firm wraps of thread to form the bullet head and flare the wing. The wing should rise away from the hook in a wide V-shape.

Blue-Winged Olive (no hackle)
as tied by Karl Kaufman

The blue-winged olive is a common north-country mayfly, especially in late summer and autumn.

Hook   Light wire, #14–#20.

Tail   Six microfibetts, divided, with three per side.

Body   Olive dubbing.

Wing   Matched grey mallard quill.

Notes   Make one turn with the dubbing, then tie in the tail. Use the dubbing to divide the tail. Then wrap the dubbing forward to the wing. Tie in the quill wings. Then wrap the dubbing forward to the head.

Bucktail Hex
as tied by Shawn Perich

This fly is easy to tie and floats well, although it tends to become waterlogged after you catch two or three fish. Once it dries, you can use it again.

Hook   Light wire, #8.

Tail   A healthy clump of yellow bucktail, somewhat longer than the hook.

Body   Yellow bucktail wrapped to the hook shank.

Wing   Yellow bucktail.

Hackle   Blue dun, palmered the length of the hook.

Notes   The tail, body and wing are made from the same clump of bucktail. Use a hair stacker to even out the tips. Secure the tail just above the bend in the hook, then wrap forward to make the body. Flare the butt ends to form the wing and trim to the correctly proportioned length. Make the palmered hackle from a single saddle hackle.

Bullet-Head Compara Hex
as tied by Dick Berge

Aside from the tail, this fly is constructed entirely of deer hair.

Hook   Light-wire, #8.

Tail   Moose mane.

Body   An extended body made of deer hair.

Wing   Deer hair.

Head   Deer hair.

Notes   For instructions for tying the bullet head and wing, see Black Hex.

Deer Hair Hex
as tied by Dave Asproth

Dave's fly is one of the few Hex patterns that doesn't incorporate an extended body.

Hook Long-shanked #10.

Tail Light-colored deer hair.

Body Light-colored deer hair, with olive poly yarn pulled over the top.

Hackle Brown and grizzly mixed or blue dun.

Notes One clump of deer hair is used to make the tail and body. Secure the clump with tips extending for the tail above the hook bend. Tie in a thin piece of poly yarn. The yarn should run along the dorsal. Secure the deer hair and yarn with tight wraps of thread.

Egg Carton Emerger
as tied by Dave Asproth

Early in the Hex hatch, an emerger riding in the surface film will sometimes outproduce a high-floating dun.

Hook #8 long-shanked dry fly hook.

Thread A light-colored thread is preferred.

Tail Natural deer hair below, olive bucktail above.

Body Yellow closed-cell foam cut from an egg carton, with olive deer hair pulled over the top.

Wing Sparse brown bucktail (optional).

Case Heart-shaped yellow closed-cell foam for wing case.

Collar Sparse deer hair.

Head Butt ends of the deer hair collar clipped to form a small, muddler-style head.

Notes When you tie in the tail, don't clip the butt ends of the olive deer bucktail. The ends should reach at least to the eye of the hook.

To make the body, cut an oval-shaped piece of foam about 1/4 inch wide and three quarters the length of the hook shank. Make a lengthwise crease in the center of the foam and fold it over the hook shank, with the fold to the bottom. Secure the foam at the base of the tail with thread. Then pull the olive deer hair butt ends from the tail forward over the top of the body. Wrap forward with thread to secure the foam and bucktail, spacing the wraps to create a segmented body.

Make the wing case by cutting a heart-shaped piece of foam and folding it lengthwise, then tying it over the body to represent developing wings. Trim the deer hair collar and head flat across the bottom so the fly rides upright in the surface film.

Elk Hair Caddis
as tied by Karl Kaufman

Caddis flies are a prevalent insect in lakes and streams. Try this fly when fish are rising sporadically.

Hook   Light wire, #12–#16.

Body   Grey dubbing.

Hackle   Ginger hackle palmered along the hook shank.

Wing   About twenty strands of fine elk hair.

Notes   Caddis have tent-shaped wings, so the elk hair wing should extend slightly past the hook bend. Trim the butt ends very short to form a small head.

Foam Body Parachute
as tied by Dave Asproth

Unlike most foam Hex patterns, this fly doesn't have an extended body.

Hook   Light-wire, #6–#8.

Tail   Two moose mane fibers.

Body   White packing foam, tinted with a dark-colored, marking pen.

Wing   Olive deer hair for the wing and hackle post.

Hackle   One olive hackle and one cream hackle, wrapped parachute-style.

Notes   Cut the foam material in thin strips and wrap it around the hook. Color the dorsal portion with a dark marking pen. To stiffen the hackle post, use a short stub of copper wire.

Foam Body Dun
as tied by Dave Asproth

Hook   Long-shanked #8.

Tail   Two long fibers from a ring-necked pheasant tailfeather.

Body   White packing foam, with a strip of gray yarn along the dorsal.

Wing   Two dozen moose mane fibers, sweeping back above the body.

Hackle   Bushy olive hackle.

Notes   After tying in the tail, secure a thin strip of gray yarn at the base of the tail. Cut a strip of foam, secure it in the same place, and wrap it around the shank to form a slim, tapered body. Pull the yarn over the top of the body and secure with wraps of thread that also form body segments. Tie in the wing, wrap the hackle, and then pull the gray yarn over the hackle like a wing case.

Foam Body Spinner
Gary Borger style
as tied by Dick Berge

The trimmed parachute hackle suggests a mayfly's spent wings.

Hook   Light wire, #8.

Tail   Three moose mane fibers.

Body   Extended body of yellow, closed-cell foam. Tint the flanks with a brown marking pen.

Hackle   Cream hackle.

Case   Cream polypropylene yarn, tinted with a brown, marking pen, for the hackle post and wing case.

Thorax   Light olive dubbing.

Notes   The tail and foam body are built on a needle. Clamp a two-inch needle in your fly-tying vise. Cut a piece of foam about 1 1/4-inch in length and 1/4-inch in diameter. Secure one end of the foam to the needle. Place three moose mane fibers lengthwise to the foam, tips extending to form a long tail. Starting at the base of the tail, wrap the thread in an "X" pattern to secure the moose mane and make a segmented body. Tighter wraps make smaller segments, so you can form a tapered body. When the body is finished, tie off with a couple of half hitches and cut the thread. Then slide the body off the needle. You'll find it convenient to make several bodies at one sitting. Tint the flanks of the finished bodies with a felt marker to match the coloration of a Hexagenia. Secure the foam body to the hook shank with wraps between the segments.

Foam Wrap Hex
as tied by Dick Lenski

Easy to tie and durable, the Foam Wrap Hex is a favorite of the Arrowhead Fly-fishers.

Hook   Light wire, #6–#8.

Body   Extended body made of tan foam athletic wrap (available at sport shops).

Tail   Sparse olive bucktail forming the underwing and extending beyond the body to represent the tail.

Wing   Light deer hair below, yellow deer hair above.

Notes   To make the body, cut a two-inch square of foam

athletic wrap. With a scissors, cut a shallow wedge from two opposite sides. With the trimmed sides facing lengthwise, roll the square as if you were making a cigarette. Fold the resulting cylinder in the middle and twist it into the shape of a mayfly body. Tie it to the hook shank, leaving enough room to build the wing. Then wrap back to the bend of the hook to secure the body to the shank. The foam body should extend an equal distance past the bend of the hook.

You'll only need a few strands of olive bucktail to make an underwing to represent the tail and add some stability to the fly. The tips of the light deer hair should be as long as the body. Trim the butt ends to about one-quarter-inch in length. Use a small clump of yellow deer hair. Trim the butt ends the same length as the light deer hair. Trim the tips, tapering toward the rear of the fly. The yellow adds a hint of color to the finished fly and makes it easier to see.

Goddard Caddis
as tied by Karl Kaufman

This fly is a favorite of Arrowhead fly-fishers when they fish the trout lakes along Minnesota's Gunflint Trail.

Hook Light wire, #6–#16.

Body Deer hair clipped in a teardrop shape and trimmed flat beneath for level flotation.

Hackle A few turns of ginger hackle.

Hair Wing Caddis
as tied by Dave Asproth

Dave uses this fly to imitate large caddis and stoneflies.

Hook Fine, wire, long-shanked #8.

Tail Deer hair.

Body Deer hair.

Wing Deer hair, slanting back.

Hackle Brown and grizzly hackle mixed.

Notes The tail and body are constructed from the same clump of deer hair. Wrap over the body with thread to secure it to the hook shank. The wing slants back over the body. The hackles are wrapped ahead of the wing.

Hex Dun, White Wing
as tied by Henry Haugley

This fly stays visible in low light conditions.

Hook Light wire, #8.

Tail Three moose mane fibers.

Body Yellow foam, tinted with a brown marking pen.

Wing White deer hair for wing and hackle post.

Hackle Olive, tied parachute-style.

Notes See Foam Body Spinner for instructions on making the foam body.

Hex, Foam Body Parachute
as tied by Dick Berge

Parachute flies always land in an upright position.

Tail Three moose mane fibers.

Body Yellow foam, tinted with a brown marking pen.

Wing Elk hair for wing and hackle post.

Hackle Grizzly tied parachute-style.

Humpy
as tied by Karl Kaufman

The Humpy is a good, all-around dry fly for trout. You can use this durable, high-floating pattern in streams or lakes.

Hook Light wire, #12–#16.

Tail Deer hair.

Body Red floss underbody with deer hair pulled over the top.

Wing White calf tail.

Hackle One brown hackle and one grizzly hackle.

Poly Wing Spinner
as tied by Dick Berge

Like a dead or dying natural mayfly, this pattern floats spread-eagle on the water.

Hook Light wire, #6.

Tail Moose mane.

Body Deer hair, tied as an extended body.

Wing Poly yarn, tied spent-wing.

Hackle Olive grizzly, equal to the width of the hook gap.

Head Tan dubbing.

Quick Caddis
as tied by Shawn Perich

Caddis flies are so prevalent in the northern waters that this fly usually catches trout whenever they're feeding on the surface. The wood duck wing seems more effective for still water and quiet streams than the elk hair wing used in some caddis patterns. This fly can be tied in various colors to match natural caddis.

Hook #12–#16 dry fly hook.

Body Sparse fur dubbing.

Wing Wood duck flank feather fibers tied flat to the hook shank.

Hackle One brown hackle wrapped ahead of the wing.

Royal Wulff
as tied by Perry Rowlison

Developed by the late Lee Wulff, Perry says this high-floating fly is one of the best attracter patterns for fast-flowing streams.

Hook Dry fly, #8–#16.

Thread Black.

Tail Brown bucktail, moose body hair for larger sizes.

Body Rear third, peacock herl; middle third, red floss; front third, peacock herl.

Wing White calf tail or white bucktail. White calf body hair in smaller sizes.

Hackle Two coachman brown hackles or one long coachman brown hackle.

Sealstead
as tied by Larry Meicher

In smaller sizes, this fly is popular with southern Wisconsin trouters. Meicher ties this large version as a

Hex imitation.

Hook Light wire, #8.

Tail A few strands of moose mane.

Body Clipped deer hair.

Wing White calf tail, tied back above the body.

Hackle Yellow.

Trico
as tied by Damian Wilmot

This fly is effective for late summer trout.

Hook #18–#22 dry fly hook.

Tail Two microfibetts.

Body #8/0 olive thread.

Thorax Black dubbing.

Hackle Two or three wraps of blue dun.

Trico Spinner
as tied by Damian Wilmot

Although it's hard to see this fly on the water, it works.

Hook #18–#22 dry fly hook.

Tail Two microfibetts.

Body Black dubbing.

Wing Sparkle-Organza fibers, tied spent wing.

WET FLIES AND NYMPHS

All Purpose Nymph
as tied by Alan Lutkevich

Al uses this pattern for trout in lakes and streams. You can also tie it in gray, olive, or other colors.

Hook Long shank, #10–#14.

Weight A few turns of lead wire.

Tail Soft ginger hackle fibers.

Body Cream fox dubbing.

Hackle Ginger hackle, about the same width as the hook gap.

Notes Dub the body from the tail to the midpoint on the hook shank. Tie in a small ginger hackle. Continue dubbing forward to the head. Then wrap the hackle forward to the head.

Caddis Pupa
as tied by Eric DiCarlo

Fish this fly with a floating line. Allow the fly to sink to the bottom, then pull it to the surface with short, fast jerks.

Hook #10–#14 wet fly hook.

Weight Lead wire.

Body Dubbed green mohair with one or two strands of Krystal Flash twisted around the dubbing.

Throat Hungarian partridge hackle mixed with three or four strands of Krystal Flash.

Candy Striper
as tied by Shawn Perich

This attracter pattern for trout has the classic red and white color combination.

Hook #8–#12 wet fly hook.

Tail Red hackle fibers.

Body Silver tinsel.

Wing White synthetic hair tied over the body and extending to the tip of the tail.

Hackle Soft, red hackle.

Casual Dress
as tied by Eric DiCarlo

This weighted nymph is a good searching pattern for trout in streams and lakes.

Hook Standard #6 wet fly hook.

Tail Red squirrel tail.

Weight Medium lead wire.

Body Dubbed rabbit fur with
the guard hairs, ribbed
with gold wire.

Head Black rabbit fur.

Copper and Herl
as tied by Shawn Perich

This simple fly consistently catches
brook trout in lakes in Minnesota's
Arrowhead country during May
and early June.

Hook A #12 wet fly hook.

Tail A few olive hackle strands.

Body Peacock herl ribbed with
medium copper wire.

Hackle Two turns of olive hen
hackle.

Dave's Red Fox Squirrel Nymph
as tied by Damian Wilmot

Similar to the Casual Dress, this fly
is tied entirely of fox squirrel.

Hook Long shank, #6–#10.

Weight A few turns of lead wire.

Tail Fox squirrel tail fibers.

Body Dubbing from the belly
fur of a fox squirrel with
the guard hairs removed.

Thorax Fox squirrel dubbing with
guard hairs to resemble legs.

Floating Hex Nymph
as tied by Dave Asproth

Fish the Floating Hex Nymph as

an emerger just prior to the hatch.

Tail A few fibers from a
ringneck pheasant tail
feather.

Under
Body Cream polypropolene
yarn.

Body Light yellow or cream
dubbing wrapped over the
yarn. Use a dark water-
proof marking pen to
mark the dorsal side.

Thorax Wild turkey marabou.

Case Fibers from a wild turkey
wing feather for the wing
case.

Eyes Plastic insect eyes.

Notes Wrap the underbody and
dubbing forward to the
thorax. Tie in the wing
case, and then tie in the
marabou. Continue
building the body forward
to the head. Tie in the
plastic eyes. Then pull the
wing case forward and tie
it off. Trim the wing case
so the butt ends extend
forward between the eyes.

Hex Strip Nymph
as tied by Henry Haugley

This is Henry's version of a fly he
says was originated by famed
Wisconsin fly-fisher Gary Borger.
Henry advises that you weight the
line (use sinking line or split shot)
rather than the fly.

Hook Light wire, #8.

Tail Tan rabbit guard hairs as long or longer than the hook shank.

Body Tan rabbit dubbing, including guard hairs. Use a bodkin to "pick out" the dubbing for a shaggy appearance.

Case Several strands of peacock herl for the wing case.

Near 'Nuff
as tied by Erik Swenson

Erik uses this fly in stream trout lakes during the Hex hatch.

Hook #8 wet fly hook.

Body Dubbed natural rabbit fur.

Case Ruffed grouse breast feather, cut in a V shape.

Collar A few grizzly hackle fibers.

Pass Lake (Larry's)
as tied by Larry Meicher

You can fish this fly wet or dry.

Hook Light wire, #12–#16

Tail Brown hackle fibers.

Body Black polypropylene yarn.

Wing White polypropylene yarn.

Hackle Two or three turns of brown hackle.

Pass Lake (traditional)
as tied by Alan Lutkevich

The Pass Lake is one of the north country's best known flies. Especially effective for brook trout, this fly will catch just about any fish that swims.

Hook #8–#12 wet fly hook.

Weight Several turns of lead wire.

Tail Coarse, brown hackle fibers.

Body Black chenille.

Wing White calf tail, extending to the tip of the tail.

Hackle Two or three turns of soft, brown hackle.

Pass Lake Hex
as tied by Larry Meicher

Leave it to the "Pass Lake Kid" to come up with this one.

Hook #8 wet fly hook.

Tail Several moose mane fibers.

Body Black polypropylene yarn.

Wing White calf tail.

Hackle Two or three turns of yellow hackle.

Possum Nymph
as tied by Shawn Perich

This is an effective general purpose nymph for smallmouth and trout in moving water.

Hook   #6–#10 nymph hook.

Tail   Badger hackle fibers.

Body   Dubbed Australian opossum, picked out with a bodkin.

Rib   Medium copper wire.

Hackle   Soft badger hackle, tied sparse.

Pheasant Tail Nymph
as tied by Karl Kaufman

Hook   #12–#16 nymph hook.

Tail   Two fibers from a ring-neck pheasant tail.

Body   Fibers from a ringneck pheasant tail, wrapped as herl.

Thorax   Peacock herl.

Case   For the wing case, one strand of gold tinsel, pulled over the top of the thorax.

Scarlet Pimp
as tied by Dave Asproth

Rainbows in lakes really go for this one.

Hook   #8 or #10 wet fly hook.

Tail   Fibers from a ringneck pheasant tail feather, as long as the fly body.

Body   Red floss wrapped to form an oval body shape.

Hackle   Brown hackle palmered the length of the hook.

Case   For the wing case, fibers from a ringneck pheasant tail feather, pulled over the body from the tail to the head.

Notes   Tie in the floss and the hackle. Secure an eight-inch loop of thread above the hook bend. Build the floss body and wrap the hackle. Tie in the fibers from a pheasant tail feather at the head. Pull the fibers back over the fly. Use the loop of thread to tie in the fibers at the base of the tail. The pheasant fibers then form the tail.

Scud
as tied by Damian Wilmot

Common in north-country waters, scud (or freshwater shrimp) are a favored trout food.

Hook   Wet fly, #12–#16.

Body   Hare's ear dubbing, tied "scruffy."

Rib   Fine gold wire.

Back   A strip of cellophane, tied in at the hook bend and pulled over the back of the fly.

Sparkle Tail Nymph
as tied by Shawn Perich

A durable, midsummer pattern for trout in lakes. It is often very effective just prior to the Hex hatch.

Hook   #10 wet fly hook.

Tail   Eight to twelve strands of green Krystal Flash.

Body   Bright, insect green dubbing.

Rib   Copper wire.

Hackle   Hungarian partridge hackle, tied very sparse.

Whiskey Fly
as tied by Bob Nasby

Tied entirely of wild turkey marabou (hence the name), the Whiskey Fly is consistently deadly on rainbow trout in lakes. You can even fish it just under the surface during the Hex hatch as an emerger. Nasby fishes the fly unweighted, on a full-sinking line.

Hook   #6–#8 wet fly hook.

Tail   Wild turkey marabou, about the length of the hook shank.

Body   Wild turkey marabou, wrapped around the hook.

Collar   Wild turkey marabou, almost as long as the hook.

Head   One copper or black bead.

Notes   To make the body, tie in a clump of marabou ahead of the tail. Twist the marabou to make a dubbing, then wrap forward. You can add a couple of strands of Krystal Flash to the tail.

Streamers

A. B.'s Floating Muddler
as tied by Dave Asproth

Dave says this Muddler variation was first tied by the late Alec Boostrom for fishing brook trout along the Gunflint Trail. It's fooled many fish over the years.

Hook #8–#10 wet fly hook.

Tail Red marabou about 1/2-inch long.

Body Silver tinsel.

Wing About one dozen strands of natural deer hair.

Head Clipped deer hair in traditional muddler shape.

Al's Marabou Streamer
as tied by Al Larson

Al has used this fly to catch everything from crappies to trout.

Hook #10 wet fly hook.

Weight Fine lead wire (optional).

Body Cream dubbing.

Rib Silver oval tinsel.

Wing White marabou.

Head Red thread.

Epoxy Head Streamer
as tied by Eric DiCarlo

A durable fly for northern pike, this streamer will also fool other large predators.

Hook #2/0 long shank with a straight eye.

Guard For the weed guard, 30-pound monofilament looped from the hook bend to the eye.

Body Pearlescent Mylar tubing, unraveled to form the tail.

Wing Synthetic hair (green over white, or other colors) mixed with a few strands of Krystal Flash.

Head Formed five-minute epoxy.

Notes Carefully shape the epoxy before it sets. When the epoxy dries, make painted eyes.

Hackle Streamer
as tied by Bob Nasby

Bob learned this pattern while fishing for tarpon and barracuda in the Florida Keys. He uses it in the north woods for pike and muskie. You can tie it in various colors.

Hook #2/0 saltwater hook.

Tail First tie in about one dozen strands of pearlescent tinsel about 1 1/2 inches long. Next tie in about two dozen strands of silver Krystal Flash about 3 inches long.

Wing Six black saddle hackles, tied immediately ahead of the tail. Tie three to a side with the tips flaring outward.

Gills Red marabou, about one-third the length of the wings, tied outside of each wing.

Collar Soft black hackle fibers.

Eyes Hard plastic hobby eyes.

Head Black thread tapered forward to the eye of the hook.

Notes The entire fly, including the eyes, is tied on the rear one-third of the hook. This design prevents the wings from wrapping around the hook. Epoxy is used to coat the tapered head and secure the eyes.

Mink Matuka Streamer
as tied by Damian Wilmot

Damian says this is an excellent leech imitation for beaver pond brookies.

Hook Long shanked, #10.

Weight A few turns of lead wire.

Body Chenille or dubbing in various colors.

Wing A strip of mink fur tied matuka-style.

Notes The mink strip should be 1 1/2 times as long as the hook shank. Secure the strip just behind the head of the fly. Using thread or fine wire, secure the fly to the hook shank with rib-like wraps. Tie off at the hook bend. A portion of the strip should stream behind the fly like a tail.

Sparse Muddler
as tied by Eric DiCarlo

Eric reduced the famous Muddler Minnow to its most basic elements for fishing rainbows in the fast currents of the Michipicoten River. The Sparse Muddler sinks quickly in swift currents, but retains the classic sculpin silhoutte of the original.

Hook #8 standard nymph hook.

Tail Brown calf tail, tied sparse.

Weight Lead or copper wire wrapped the length of the body.

Body Gold tinsel.

Wing Brown calf tail, tied sparse, below. One clump of deer hair, above.

Head One or two clumps of deer hair, trimmed to form muddler head.

Notes Yellow calf tail is also effective. If you use copper wire for weight, the tinsel overwrap is unnecessary.

Sculpin

as tied by Dave Asproth

Dave uses this fly to catch Lake Superior brook trout in the harbor at Grand Marais, Minnesota.

Hook #4 streamer hook.

Weight Lead wire.

Tail Grizzly marabou.

Body Brown fuzzy wool ribbed with gold oval tinsel.

Fins Pectoral fins of grizzly marabou.

Collar Deer hair.

Head Clipped deer hair.

Eyes Preformed plastic eyes.

Notes Build a tapered body with the fuzzy wool to imitate a sculpin's potbellied shape. Tie in one small grizzly marabou feather on each side of the fly to represent quivering pectoral fins. The deer hair collar should be sparse and flared wide. Tie in the plastic eyes and then build the head with several clumps of deer hair. Clip the head and collar to create a profile that is flat on the bottom and on the top. Sculpin have a similar profile.

Squirrel Tail

as tied by Karl Kaufman

The prominent white squirrel tail wing makes this fly a dependable attracter pattern for trout.

Hook #10–#12 wet fly hook.

Body Flat silver tinsel with oval silver tinsel rib.

Wing Gray squirrel tail.

BUGS AND CRITTERS

The Ape Series
as tied by Greg Breining

Chimpanzee

Hook   #1 or #1/0 jig hook

Weight   #3/0 split shot pinched on beneath the hook eye and fastened with epoxy.

Tail   Black marabou. A few strands of green Krystal Flash are optional.

Body   Black or dark olive chenille.

Wing   One or two clumps of black deer hair spun around the hook. Leave the butt ends long to create a bulky collar.

Hackle   Twenty to forty rubber legs about 2 inches long.

Notes   The deer hair collar will make the rubber legs bulge out, creating a bulky fly with lots of action.

Gorilla

Same pattern as the Chimpanzee, except the tail is made of marabou and four to six saddle hackles.

King Kong

The biggest fly in the ape series. Tie the same as a Chimpanzee or Gorilla. Use a #3/0 jig hook and a #7 split shot. The tail is made of ten to twelve saddle hackles.

Dahlberg Diver
as tied by Larry Dahlberg

Originally tied to fool bass, Dahlberg has caught numerous species of fish worldwide using variations of this fly.

Hook   A straight-eyed hook of standard shank length, commonly #1/0, but can be smaller or larger.

Tail   A tapered strip of rabbit fur about 1 1/2 times the length of the hook and a few strands of Flashabou.

Head Clipped deer hair. Trim the fly very flat on the bottom. The upper half should be clipped in a conical shaped that meets a stiff, deer hair collar. Shape the head carefully, because it controls the diving action of the fly.

Notes You can tie this fly in varied colors. Dahlberg prefers a rabbit-strip tail, but also makes the tail from feathers or hair. He considers a few strands of Flashabou essential. When fishing in turbid water, he uses a tail made mostly of Flashabou with some feathers or hair mixed in. Be sure to use a hook with a straight eye. Also, if the hook shank is too long, the fly will be difficult to cast.

Fox Squirrel Crayfish
as tied by Shawn Perich

This pattern imitates the shape and movement of a crayfish scuttling across the bottom. Retrieve it near the bottom with short twitches. In still water, the fly is most effectively fished with a sinking line.

Hook #2 nymph hook.

Weight Dumbbell eyes.

Tail Clump of fox squirrel tail split to form two "claws."

Body Burnt orange chenille.

Hackle One olive saddle hackle.

Notes Tie in the tail and split with figure-eight wraps. Tie in dumbbell eyes on top of the hook shank so the hook rides point up. Secure both with head cement. Tie in the butt of the saddle hackle 1/2 inch from the base of the tail. Wrap on chenille body and then wrap the hackle forward to the lead eyes. Long, webby fibers at the butt of the hackle represent the crayfish legs.

Mylar "Stickbait"
as tied by Eric DiCarlo

This fly looks like a balsa wood stick bait—a popular north-country spinning lure. An excellent fly for smallmouth bass or trout, the "Stickbait" is too fragile for pike.

Hook #2/0 light, long-shanked hook with a straight eye.

Tail Marabou.

Body Large pearlescent Mylar tubing.

Eyes Plastic doll eyes.

Notes Begin by boiling the tubing to remove any coil. Then pull the core out of the tubing.

Cut a length of tubing long enough to make two flies. Wrap a light wire around the center, forming the taper for the tail of each fly.

Use a 1/8-inch dowel to coat the inside of the tube with five-minute epoxy. It will take two or three coats to give the body sufficient stiffness. When the epoxy hardens, you can remove the wire and cut apart the tube.

Tie in the tail. Slide the tubing down the hook shank, beginning from the eye. Use silicon or epoxy to seal the tail and body.

Cut a slight taper for the head, so the fly dives when it is retrieved. Use styrofoam to plug the head cavity, sealed with epoxy.

Use epoxy to attach hobby eyes. The fly can be painted in any color pattern.

Wooly Bugger
as tied by Shawn Perich

Although it is often considered a leech imitation, the Wooly Bugger also resembles crayfish, minnows, and large nymphs that inhabit northern waters. It's an excellent searching fly for trout of all species, bass, and walleyes. My favorite color is olive, but many anglers prefer black. The recipe below is for an olive fly. It is followed by variations suggested by other anglers.

Hook #10–#14 streamer hook

Tail Olive marabou slightly longer than the hook, with four to eight strands of green Crystal Flash.

Weight Six turns of medium copper wire.

Body Olive chenille wrapped almost to the eye of the hook.

Hackle Olive saddle hackle. Tie in the tip of the hackle ahead of the tail and palmer forward the length of the body. Use a soft, webby hackle to create a "buggy" appearance.

Notes Wrap the weight forward from the center of the hook. This will give your fly an undulating action. You can also weight the fly with dumbbell eyes.

Black Wooly Bugger
as tied by Karl Kaufman

The marabou, chenille, and hackle should be black. The Black Wooly Bugger will catch just about anything that swims. In small sizes (#10–#12) this is a great early-season trout fly.

Black Wooly Bugger
as tied by Dave Asproth

The marabou, hackle and chenille are black. Add a few strands of copper tinsel in the tail. Wrap in copper tinsel just behind the head. Finish the head by tying in plastic eyes. Dave says he's caught brook trout on this fly just about every place he's tried it.

Dick's Spinner Fly
as tied by Dick Lenski

Tie an eighteen-inch, six-pound, monofilament leader to any Wooly Bugger. Thread three or four fluorescent beads on the leader,

then add a small, French-style spinner on a clevis. Thread one more bead ahead of the spinner.

Holschlag Hackle Fly
as tied by Tim Holschlag

Add three or four pairs of yellow or white rubber legs to a standard Wooly Bugger. The legs should be about 3/4 inch long and stiff enough to "swim" when the fly is retrieved. Weight the fly with dumbbell eyes. Tim Holschlag says this fly is an effective crayfish imitation for smallmouth that sometimes outproduces a Wooly Bugger by three to one.

Ice Bugger
as tied by Tim Holschlag

Use plastic Ice Chenille for the body to create a translucent Wooly Bugger.

Sparkle Bugger
as tied by Shawn Perich

This is a big fly. Use a #2 hook. Tie a Black Wooly Bugger with a body of gold tinsel chenille. Add bead chain or dumbbell eyes so the hook rides with the point up. Try this version for big brown trout, smallmouth in rivers, or large-mouth and pike in lakes.

Yellow Wooly Bugger (modified)
as tied by Bob Nasby

Tie in a yellow marabou tail with a few strands of red Krystal Flash. Make the body from yellow or light green Ice Chenille. Tie in a collar of soft yellow hackle. Finish the fly with a gold bead head. This is Bob's favorite Hex nymph.

The Working Man's Popper
as tied by Eric Dicarlo

A durable popper for pike, muskie, and largemouth bass that's made from materials you can find at a discount store. Effective color combinations include black and fluorescent orange (or chartreuse) and red and white.

Hook	#2/0 light, long-shanked hook with a straight eye, such as an inexpensive bait hook.
Tail	Synthetic hair about 6 inches long below. Six to eight saddle hackles above.
Head	Dense closed-cell foam carved in a wedge shape. Cut a slit for the hook shank and fasten to the hook with epoxy.
Guard	For the weed guard, cut two 2-inch lengths of heavy monofilament from a weed-trimming machine. Insert into the foam so the monofilament curves back to the hook point.

Index